THUNDER OVER KASHMIR

Frontispiece The air lift

THUNDER OVER KASHMIR

LT.-COL. MAURICE COHEN
(The Corps of Signals)

With a Foreword by
Lieut.-General K. S. Thimayya, D.S.O.

Orient BlackSwan

THUNDER OVER KASHMIR

ORIENT BLACKSWAN PRIVATE LIMITED

Registered Office
3-6-752 Himayatnagar, Hyderabad 500 029, Telangana, India
e-mail: centraloffice@orientblackswan.com

Other Offices
Bengaluru, Chennai, Guwahati, Hyderabad, Kolkata, Mumbai, New Delhi, Noida, Patna, Visakhapatnam

First published by Orient Blackswan Private Limited 1955
Reprinted 1994, 1995
First Orient Blackswan impression 2011
Reprinted 2012, 2022

ISBN 978-81-250-0016-7

Typeset by
Alliance Phototypesetters, Pondicherry 605 013

035441

Printed in India at
Glorious Printers, Delhi 110 095

Published by
Orient Blackswan Private Limited
3-6-752, Himayatnagar, Hyderabad 500 029, Telangana, India
e-mail: info@orientblackswan.com

Dedicated
To Those Who Fell

Foreword

I HAVE great pleasure in writing this foreword for Lt. Col. Maurice Cohen. A book of this type is long over-due in respect of the operation carried out by the Indian Army in Jammu & Kashmir. Not only was the Indian Army faced with a stupendous task in October 1947, but the way they faced those difficulties and carried out their subsequent operations will go down as an epic in the annals of the history of free India.

Lieutenant Colonel Cohen's book has been written in simple and soldierly language. It will be followed not only by the officers of the Army but also by the average civilian who may not understand the technique and tactics of war. I congratulate the author on this effort of his and wish him every success.

K. S. Thimayya,
Lt. Gen.

Contents

Foreword

KASHMIR AGLOW 1

POONCH 9

THE ISOLATED CITY 15

GENERAL THIMAYYA REORGANISES 26

A RESTLESS MONTH 33

THE BREAK-THROUGH 39

INTERIM PERIOD—JULY TO SEPTEMBER 52

PRELIMINARY BLOWS 63

19 BRIGADE MOVES OUT 79

INTO THE FRAY 88

THE ROAD GOES THROUGH 104

Index 113

Plates

Between pages 14 and 15

Sardar Patel, with leaders of Kashmir, Sheikh Abdullah and Ghulam Mohammed.
Lt. Col. D. R. Rai, M.V.C. (Posthumous).
Brig. Mohammed Usman, M.V.C. (Posthumous).
Lieutenant General Cariappa and Lieutenant General Srinagesh.
The solitary sentinel.
Mountain warfare.
Amongst the clouds and still climbing.
Return from a small operation.
A village burning. Will Poonch have the same fate?

Between pages 28 and 29

The Prime Minister at Jammu with Maj. Gen. Atma Singh.
The Prime Minister at the Festival in Srinagar.
Gen. Kulwant Singh, Brigadier Sen and Lt. Col. (later Brigadier) Harbaksh Singh engrossed in plans.
Major General Thimayya with Lieutenant General Srinagesh and UNO Officials.

Between pages 40 and 41

Regimental signallers leading.
A wireless set on pack transport.
Flying Officer D. Barty.
The Muletter taking supplies to the Picquets.
Before the Beripattan Bridge was built.
Beripattan Bridge being opened.
A Flying trolley.
Crossing the river Munawwarwati.

Between pages 78 and 79

On the way to Thana Mandi. Armour goes into action.
The author outside signal officer bunker.
Artillery training.
Lieutenant General Srinagesh inspecting an armoured column.
A respite.

Maj. Gen. Atma Singh, Brigadier (the late Major General) Khanolkar, Major Lee (UNO), and Major Lamba.
The Yuvaraj and the Yuvarani with Sheikh Abdullah.
Maj. Gen. Atma Singh and Brig. Yadunath Singh.

Between pages 98 and 99

A welcome invasion.
A moment of cheer in Kashmir
Congratulations from Maj. Gen. Atma Singh to Brig. Yadunath Singh.

1

Kashmir Aglow

THE harsh reality of modern war is seldom thrust upon a peace-loving country with any warning. It comes suddenly and unexpectedly, and unless she is well prepared to meet a sudden onslaught the attacker will get the advantages of surprise and initial momentum, advantages which may well prove overwhelming. Even in relatively normal times no country having peaceful intentions likes to spend its national wealth and energy on massive defence forces. But when times are not normal, when there is a fear of aggression, when internal resources are strained by poverty or political crisis, it is still more difficult for a country to bear the strain of modern war.

In the last quarter of 1947 times were not normal in India. In the joy of her newly won Independence, she was still in the throes of Partition; she was having to quell communal disorders of gigantic scale; she had millions of refugees, displaced by the partition of the country, to keep alive by whatever relief she could give them; she was short of food and short of money; even her defence services with their material and equipment were in process of being divided and shared with the new state on her borders. Never for a moment did it occur to her that at the very birth of her freedom she would have to defend herself against unprovoked and undeclared attack. In a flash, and without any warning, war burst upon Kashmir.

The Invasion

On 22 October, 1947 large bands of raiders poured across the border from Pakistan into Kashmir and Jammu at several points. They came in motor vehicles and were armed with modern weapons including Bren guns, heavy mortars, anti-tank rifles, grenades and land mines and they seemed to have an unlimited supply of ammunition. They were led by officers fully conversant with modern strategy and warfare. They came attracted by prospects, indeed promises, of loot.

The main column of the raiders drove down the Domel–Baramula road heading for Srinagar, their main objective. They soon overwhelmed the resistance put up by the small Kashmir State Forces and within four days of crossing the border they had captured the electric power station at Mahura, fifty miles from Srinagar, plunging Srinagar into darkness, and threatened both Baramula and Srinagar itself. Other columns crossed the border further south, in the districts of Poonch and Mirpur.

The Momentous Decision

At the time of Partition the State of Jammu and Kashmir had acceded neither to Pakistan nor to India; a Standstill Agreement, however, had been signed between the Kashmir Government and Pakistan. The invasion having come from within Pakistan, the Maharaja of Kashmir had no alternative but to seek India's assistance. On 25 October he sent an S.O.S. to the Government of India seeking military help and offering to accede to the Indian Union. The next day he signed the Instrument of Accession and the Government of India took the momentous decision to rush troops to the defence of Kashmir. A hastily-improvised airlift was whirled into operation. As it turned out, this was only just in the nick of time, for when on 27 October the first batch of Indian troops, consisting of three companies under the command of Lt. Col. D. R. Rai, landed at Srinagar aerodrome the enemy were in the immediate vicinity. A few minutes later the airfield might well have been in enemy hands.

Very quickly, over a hundred civil aircraft, all Dakotas, were mobilised to fly troops, equipment and supplies to Srinagar. Indian civil pilots and crews rose manfully to the occasion and worked day and night to make this epic air operation a success, for the air was the only practicable highway. Over three hundred miles of broken mountainous track formed the only land link between Srinagar and India. Though later improved, this road still remains a far from ideal line of communication for the Indian troops in Kashmir.

A flight forming part of the first airlift has been graphically described by Maj. (now Lieutenant Colonel) L. E. R. B. Ferris, who was Brigade Major of 161 Bde.: "The air flight to the valley of Kashmir was a nightmare. There was no information of any sort available as to what exactly was happening, where the raiders were, what was the plan of action, what personal kit was due to be taken and a hundred other queries which remained unanswered. In short we just did not know what to expect." (It must be remembered that the Commander-in-Chief had taken immediate action and troops started to move within ten hours of the decision to help Kashmir, and this in spite of the disorganised state of the Army consequent upon Partition. The Army was dispersed over a wide area, helping to cope with the riots and refugees; and several battalions were still in Pakistan as far away as the North-West Frontier.) Ferris continues: "Aircraft from the various civil aviation lines were pressed into service. The luxury fittings were ripped out, comfortable chairs pulled out of their fixtures, and within minutes fully-armed troops clambered aboard—as many as could fit in. This was the scene that was repeated several times a day at the Willingdon Airport, New Delhi. The flight itself was uneventful. One had to squat on the deck of the Dakota and from such a position the windows were too high to look out and see the countryside below. The pilots were a fine lot. They invariably took us singly into their cockpit and let us see what we were flying over. One saw long strings of refugee caravans, and dotted below was an odd house or village still smouldering. As soon as the news that the aircraft was nearing Jammu filtered through the hatchway leading from the air crew to the passengers' hold, there was a surge of activity. The troops all took up their weapons, buttoned up their ammunition pouches, adjusted their equipment and stood up ready to move. The Dakota lurched and bumped, and as it banked over the landing-ground tossed men against each other and against the sides of the hold.

"On landing we were told that Jammu was not our destination, but Srinagar. After a short respite when we got out of the aircraft to stretch our legs and smoke a cigarette, we emplaned—or rather jumped aboard, as there were no ramps. The journey to Srinagar took 45 minutes and it was pleasant to see the snow on the Pir Punjal and just a little freshly-fallen snow on the Banihal Pass. Everything appeared so picturesque, calm and peaceful-looking out of that Dakota window. Soon we were circling over the landing strip at Srinagar—as landing was difficult due to the mist below.

"At last the plane settled. We jumped out of the Dakota and for a moment we wondered what it was all about. Was it training or was it actually the real thing? It was not until we heard the sound of small-arms and machine-gun fire and saw one or two of our men wounded by bullets that ricochetted that we realised that we had run into it. We did not even have time to look around us before we were assembled together, jointly briefed and launched straight out into battle."

Not often in the history of warfare has an operation been put through with so little pre-planning and with so many handicaps, not the least of which were almost non-existent lines of communication, a complete lack of intelligence of enemy strength and disposition, and a meagre knowledge of the country and terrain, for a detailed survey of the area had yet to be made.

Colonel Rai, the Commanding Officer of the first battalion to land, had to make a quick decision. By now the enemy was already in Baramula, the strategic bottleneck that controls the Srinagar valley. If once the invaders were allowed to enter and fan out into the Srinagar plain, there would be little hope left. Should he, with only four hundred men, give battle to the invaders who were estimated to number anything from two to five thousand, or should he await reinforcements? The latter course might have proved fatal as the enemy would, in all probability, have reached Srinagar.

Taking the initiative, he crashed headlong into the invader's column with only two companies, leaving the third to guard the aerodrome. Heavy casualties were suffered on both sides, Colonel Rai himself falling mortally wounded while gallantly leading his men. But the enemy was hurled back, his columns disorganised, his advance halted, and a breathing space was gained while reinforcements arrived from India. More forces were being flown into Srinagar, while armoured cars and artillery slowly wound their way along the three hundred miles of perilous road over narrow, rickety bridges from East Punjab via Jammu and the 9,290 foot Banihal Pass.

Srinagar Saved

At dawn on 7 November twelve days after the first batch of Indian troops had landed in Srinagar—the Indian Army went over to the offensive with three battalions and a squadron of armoured cars. The engagement, which took place barely four miles from the city, lasted twelve hours, at the end of which the invaders fled in utter disorder, leaving about 500 dead on the field. Next day Baramula, the key to the valley, was recaptured in the afternoon, and by 14 November the raiders had been chased beyond Uri, 65 miles from Srinagar.

A few days later we learnt that in Gilgit, in the far north of Kashmir an insurgent group had staged a local *coup d'état* and after imprisoning the Governor, had established its own regime. There was now a threat from the north too.

Jammu Province

In the meantime the situation in Jammu, to the south, was causing anxiety for through it ran our only land link with India—the rough, difficult mountain road along which all our heavy transport and equipment had to come. The raiders had seized considerable areas adjacent to the Pakistan border. The fact that they did not cut the road may have been due to a number of causes: their main pre-occupation with the Kashmir valley and the prospect of richer loot in Srinagar; their possible reluctance to risk a big engagement so near to the Indian border; and above all, the determined resistance put up by the small groups of Kashmir State Forces and the local population who together held the first onrush. In the districts of Mirpur, Muzaffarabad, Poonch and part of Riasi our aircraft on reconnaissance spotted fires raging in the villages overrun by the enemy. It soon became clear that the State Forces, which had taken up positions in key towns near the Jammu–Pakistan border, were surrounded in Mirpur, Kotli, Poonch, Jhangar, Naushera, Bhimbar, Rajauri and Beripattan.

What Indian troops could be spared were diverted towards these beleaguered towns in Jammu, to relieve the hard-pressed garrisons and save the lives of the thousands of refugees from the countryside, mainly women and children, sheltering there. Our troops first relieved Beripattan and then Naushera and Jhangar, while a column sent to Kotli succeeded in evacuating the garrison and bringing about 9,000 refugees out to safety. Owing to lack of troops the garrison at Mirpur could not be relieved, but it later fought its way out, bringing thousands of refugees with it.

As winter set in with all its severity, it froze up the fronts in the Valley of Kashmir, but in the less severe conditions in Jammu fighting flared up on a bigger scale. Going over to the offensive, our troops operating near Naushera captured the enemy stronghold of Kot on 1 February, and that of Kaman Gosha Gali soon after. Five days later the biggest battle of the Kashmir campaign took place. Gathering a force of some 6,000 men, the enemy mounted a three-pronged attack on Naushera on 6 February. The Indian force was commanded by the gallant Brig. Mohammad Usman. The battle lasted two days. Wave after wave of the enemy attacked our perimeter and severe hand-to-hand fighting developed. The heavy casualties suffered by the raiders were the measure of their determination to wrest back this strategic town. The enemy was eventually routed, leaving about 2,000 killed and having many more wounded. Our casualties were comparatively light.

Following this success, our troops recaptured Jhangar on 18 March, losing only twelve men in the action as against the enemy's 300 in killed alone, thus avenging the loss of this place three months before when the enemy overwhelmed a small force of Indian troops consisting of about two companies. Jhangar is situated at the point where the road forks to Kotli and Mirpur; its recapture was thus an important strategic gain.

The Story of Poonch Unfolds

It is here that the story of Poonch unfolds. I have chosen to make it the central theme of this book because I am sure that as time goes on the epic of its defence and its ultimate relief will become more and more a source of pride to the people of India and will not fail to stir the imagination of the rest of the world. Whenever a beleaguered garrison holds out against overwhelming odds a feeling of admiration is kindled in every but the most ignoble heart. In this particular episode the city of Poonch, with forty-five thousand people, mainly women and children, within its improvised defences, was beset on all sides by a ruthless enemy, bent upon loot and rapine of the most savage nature.

Had Poonch fallen the consequences would have been serious indeed. First there was the fate of her inhabitants; judging from the bitter experiences of the people of Baramula, Uri and other towns overrun by the enemy, its capture would have brought horror and misery worse than death, such as had befallen the womenfolk in those unfortunate places and such as they alone could have endured. It is this that makes the story of the battle for Poonch something more than a mere fight for positional supremacy and gives it as human a touch as can be found in the annals of warfare.

Secondly, quite apart from the effect on its own garrison and inhabitants, the fall of Poonch would have had grave military repercussions. Once in possession of Poonch and of its surrounding hills the enemy would have been free to harass our lines of communications and main supply route to such an extent that the effectiveness of the whole campaign, particularly in the Kashmir Valley, would have been jeopardised.

Finally, the story of Poonch gives us a fairly typical picture of the conditions under which this whole campaign was fought. The type of warfare, the mountainous terrain, the problems of communication and supply, the experiences of the soldier and civilian alike—all were much the same round Poonch as anywhere else in the State; for Poonch is in the very heart of Kashmir.

2

Poonch

THE men and women of Poonch are well known as a sturdy and courageous people. The women have a stately bearing and their renowned Kashmir beauty is marked by a charm and grace that is enhanced by the natural surroundings of their homeland. Their fair skins and Grecian features contrast sharply with the rugged beauty of the barren hills. The fame of their loveliness has spread far beyond the confines of their homeland and has been immortalised in the sculptural genius and poetic art of the nation to which they belong. Yet, in spite of this, they remain daughters of the soil, following their menfolk to the fields, ministering to their domestic needs and living in the sheltering shadows of community life.

The men of Poonch, tall, lithe and hardy, their lives similarly secluded, hemmed in by a part of the massive Himalayan range, go about their daily tasks minding their own business, neither caring, nor giving much thought for affairs of the outside world. Occasionally one or other of Poonch's sons ventures beyond the natural barriers of his own small world and returns with tales of lives lived differently from his own. But such tales, once told, are forgotten; for they fall on the ears of a people who live within themselves and are content with what they have and hold. And who will blame them? For are not their fields the same fields their ancestors have tilled and toiled in for generations past and have now entrusted to their care? They need no more. So they listen patiently to the tales told to them, nodding wisely, as though they understand, and go back to their ploughs to till once more the good earth their fathers and forefathers lived and died upon. Their code of life, silent and unvoiced, is built upon one thought—"to live and let live, each unto his own"—a common saying, a noble thought.

In normal times Kashmir is a state as peaceful and calm as the clear still waters of its lily-shrouded lakes; and Poonch is a state within a state, its own slumbering tranquillity contributing to the peacefulness of the whole. Such was the situation in this area when the holocaust was unleashed.

What then would have happened to the people had circumstances turned out otherwise and had the invaders captured their homeland in their first onslaught?

The lovely women of Poonch would have been kidnapped and raped or sold. Or they would have been sent to the raiders in isolated picquets or in groups behind the front line to satisfy their animal passions and so provide an incentive to continue fighting. They would have suffered the same frightful experiences as their sisters suffered in Baramula, Rajauri and countless other unhappy places.

The menfolk and children would have been massacred or made to work as cattle, or used in whatever other way suited the whims of their captors. Their jewellery, silver and gold, and whatever else of value they had, would have been taken as private booty, the property of whoever first laid hands on it.

Is it any wonder, then, that the hordes running loose with visions of loot and lust before them, knocked hard and constantly at the gates of Poonch city, surrounding it on all sides, cursing savagely, attacking fiendishly, and striving with one another to be the first to force a way in for the kill—and the reward.

The city of Poonch lies some 45 miles south-west of Srinagar and rather more than 80 miles north-west of Jammu. But though both these places were in friendly hands in the early months of 1948, the cold mountain peaks and passes that stood between the people of Poonch and their friends were held by the same cruel enemy that gazed rapaciously at the city from the surrounding heights, sustained and encouraged by the people of Pakistan whose boundary stood a mere 30 miles to the west.

The importance of Poonch and its plight was realised at the very highest level in the country and by none other than the Prime Minister of India himself.

Early in December 1947, there were a number of high-ranking civil and military officers present when the situation in Poonch was under discussion. Prime Minister Nehru, who was also present, stated that it would be most unwise even to contemplate evacuation from Poonch. The fate of refugees numbering 45,000 would be terrible. However, he hoped there would be a change for the better in the political relationship between India and Pakistan, in which case the Poonch problem would be simplified. If not, the importance of saving the population justified all the risks and hazards to be taken—and he realised there were many.

Prime Minister Nehru's main concern was the safety of the people there. But from a military point of view the fall of Poonch would have been disastrous. Nor would it have been creditable for the Indian Army were it to abandon the 45,000 men, women and children to their fate at this critical juncture.

Thus, the decision was reached that Poonch would be defended at all costs. The matter was confirmed by the Prime Minister to his colleagues. Sardar Vallabhbhai Patel, the Deputy Prime Minister, nodded in full agreement and with no little satisfaction, for thereby he was expressing his own personal views.

Mountain Warfare

The problem that faced the Indian forces, not only in Poonch but wherever they were fighting in Kashmir, was not only the problem of a ruthless enemy fighting largely as guerillas, but also that of wild, undeveloped and mountainous country.

Mountain warfare is primarily a battle for heights. In general, the higher the feature captured the more securely can the position be maintained, for the very fact of its height and the steep climb up to it, is a natural defence that the opposition forces must overcome. Add to this a blasting fire of machine guns, rifles and grenades, all bearing down from above, and the problem of attacking such a height becomes a grave and dangerous one.

Yet to rely on a hill mainly because of its altitude is suicidal for the defenders. To consolidate the main position its flanks must be protected and the approaches kept under close observation.

A force making for a particular objective in mountainous country advances by leap-frogging its formations, at the same time keeping a watch on both sides of the route and maintaining direct contact with its headquarters, usually by radio. And when halted, either by day or by night, whether in a vulnerable valley or on a dominating hill feature, it is asking for trouble to neglect placing picquets on nearby heights from which the surrounding country can be watched. Otherwise, enemy parties may reach the top of those same hills by climbing, unseen, up the far slopes. Then they may be in a position to cause considerable damage with such weapons as mortars. Similarly the enemy may collect undetected on the far side of a nearby hill and make a sudden and unexpected raid resulting in loss to men and materials and be off before a counter-attack can be organised.

In this type of warfare one of the greatest handicaps is the lack of roads and railways. In Jammu and Kashmir there are a few roads and no railways. One has therefore to decide how much equipment is to be considered essential and how much can be sacrificed for swift movement, which is of the greatest importance. Ability to switch from one place to another without loss of time on difficult ground is a great advantage in a mountainous country; and superior marching power, endurance, sound organisation, and light equipment all contribute to speedy movement.

Mobility, though so important, is of little value unless it is backed up with sufficient fire power. Here again it is the question of the right kind of weapons; well-trained mountain artillery, which can switch its guns from one place to another in the shortest time, is of immense value.

The third important factor in mountain warfare—and it is one which can often be the deciding factor—is the individual, the soldier himself. In orthodox warfare the machine plays such a big part that the individual man is less important—he is only necessary as a part of the whole machine. But when campaigning in the Himalayas, where Nature provides natural defence, the task requires a standard of individual fitness, specially in attack, that has no equal in any other kind of warfare. To be able to cross obstacles on foot and scale precipices, crests and peaks, some higher even than the clouds, is a great test of endurance. And in addition to stamina the soldier must possess determination and be able to remain continually alert. He has to climb like a cat upwinding mountain passes, keeping low to avoid shelling and machine-gun fire. Not only does this demand the highest standard of physical toughness but a generous measure of mental efficiency is also necessary. The individual man must have not only a will to reach the objective, but absolute determination to seize and hold on to the position. Then only is a soldier psychologically ready for the fight. If will and determination combined with stamina and mental alertness are absent in a man, then the mountains are no place for that man to fight—they would only tear out his heart. Though the fighting in Jammu and Kashmir never reached the same tempo as that of battles that have been fought in Sicily, Tunisia and North Korea, and though we have no enemy air power against us, the fighting was invariably furious and tough; and since the country was suited mainly for defence, success in attack was not easy to achieve.

During the last World War, General Eisenhower once said that in the mountains of Italy a battalion could stop an Army's advance (an American Army is sixty times more powerful than a battalion). But none of the heights in Italy have an altitude of more than five or six thousand feet whereas in the Kashmir Himalayas one seems to be surrounded by an endless sea of mountain ranges rising and falling in massive waves reaching over 20,000 ft. in height and snow-capped throughout the year. Even Srinagar, which stands 5,000 ft. above sea level, lies in the midst of a vale walled in on all sides by towering mountains.

One of the last features captured by our *jawans* in the Kashmir operations was 17,400 ft. high. This mountain-top was taken against a raging Himalayan blizzard sweeping like a hurricane at over a hundred miles an hour. At this altitude even seasoned mountaineers from Europe moving at their own pace with all the latest scientific aids avoid climbing without the use of oxygen. Here the temperature falls so low that if marching troops halt on a hillside for only ten minutes they risk getting frozen.

It is no exaggeration to say that the Kashmir campaign was one of almost unequalled strain for the individual soldier. But there was, as in all mountain warfare, one advantage. For one principle of this kind of fighting is that the higher the feature held the more secure it is. The massive heights are in themselves a natural and formidable fortification of defence and once such positions are secured they provide an excellent springboard for launching an offensive.

Sardar Patel with leaders of Kashmir: Sheikh Abdullah, the Prime Minister
and Bakshi Ghulam Mohammed, the Deputy Prime Minister

Lt. Col. D. R. Rai, M.V.C. (Posthumous)
Killed in action

Brig. Mohammed Usman, M.V.C.
(Posthumous)

General Cariappa and General Srinagesh. From success to success

The solitary sentinel

Mountain warfare

Amongst the clouds and still climbing

Return from a small operation

A village burning. Will Poonch have the same fate?

3

The Isolated City

WHEN I officially went into Kashmir, I was the Officer Commanding 3 Company as a Major in 2 Airborne Divisional Signal Regiment. But even earlier than this, in fact since February 1948, about three months after the Kashmir struggle had begun, I had been at Pathankot railhead on the Kashmir–India border.

I had been appointed to raise the nucleus of the Srinagar Divisional Signal Regiment at Pathankot, later redesignated 19 Divisional Signal Regiment, which played so important a rôle in Kashmir. While in this appointment I paid a visit to Jammu and from there took a trip with Flt. Lt. T. Wynne to Poonch. At the headquarters in Poonch, I met Brig. Pritam Singh, Major Suleman—the Medical Officer, now a Lieutenant Colonel—and several other officers and civilians. It was partly from them that I got eyewitness accounts, and partly as a result of my own observation that I got a first-hand picture of the events described in this chapter, which took place between November 1947 and February 1948. At the time I had no idea that I would soon be taking an active part in the operations around this very area of Poonch.

At first there had been confusion within the walls of Poonch city. Forty thousand men, women and children were crowded into the small area of ten square miles, which had never held before more than eight thousand inhabitants. Many had arrived there in panic, fleeing before the oncoming invaders whose presence in the area was made evident from miles away by the smoke of burning villages. No one can say why these refugees had poured into Poonch city, for it was very obvious that there could not be enough food to feed even half of them.

In Srinagar, the capital of the State, and in other more fortunate places of Kashmir, Poonch would be talked about in those days in a hushed voice. It was thought of as a doomed city and those who spoke of it felt in their hearts that they had seen for the last time their friends and relatives who were among those forty thousand.

When the siege began there were two depleted battalions of the Kashmir State Forces—a total of scarcely 1200 men—to defend the city. These troops, mustering all the arms and ammunition they could, spent the early days of the battle rushing from hill to hill and from summit to summit in a semi-exhausted stupor, defending wherever the enemy attacked with whatever energy they had left; and they just managed to hold out. To these brave men, to fall at the point of the sword was of little consequence, but to surrender or to allow the raiders to break through seemed worse than death.

These men had no contact with the outside world, not even with Srinagar, their Base Headquarters, for they lacked radio equipment. There were no communications and no news came from them except for occasional tales which trickled out with individuals who escaped. The men of Poonch were fighting as a separate entity and, as one officer said, "There was always a prayer on our lips which was not only for ourselves."

The Indian Army Enters

Such was the state of affairs when the Indian Army, less than 24 hours after the first orders had been passed, made their dramatic entry into Kashmir by air.

Then, knowing full well the plight of the people of Poonch, a column was detached and, wheeling swiftly to the left after capturing Baramula and Uri, proceeded south to the relief of the city. Their vehicles crossed high mountain ranges covered with thick jungle—ideal country for ambush—through the Haji Pir Pass, 8000 ft. high. The troops allotted for this push formed part of 161 Infantry Brigade under the leadership of Brig. L. P. Sen, D.S.O. and included battalions of the well-known Dogra and Sikh regiments. They were supported by a squadron of armoured cars commanded by Maj. P. K. Kuriyan, who was later awarded the Vir Chakra for his gallantry and dash in action.

But even this relieving column had no communication with the beleaguered garrison of Poonch. The result was most unfortunate, for the over-cautious defenders, sighting from their summits a column of troops heading towards the city in those days of complete uncertainty, feared that they were raiders and so blew up the bridge at Kahuta, eight miles from Poonch, thus cutting themselves off completely from the only land link with Uri and Srinagar and from what would have been a free flow of men and supplies.

The relieving troops were, however, determined to fulfil their task. The leading unit of a parachute battalion of the famous Kumaon Regiment fought as normal infantry under the command of Lt. Col. Pritam Singh and succeeded in crossing the fast-rising river with all its equipment. Then, with frantic efforts they managed to convey to the defenders that they were Indian troops and friends and not the enemy: It was thus that the Kumaon parachutists joined hands with the Poonch garrison in the defence of the city, knowing, as they marched through the city gates, that they themselves would soon be cut off.

The remainder of the column which had come as an escort, being in a position liable to ambush and heavy attack, returned at once to Uri.

Lt. Col. Pritam Singh (now Brigadier) took over the defence of the city and soon, among friend and foe alike, became renowned as the 'Lion of Poonch'. Indeed he and his men of the Kumaon Regiment were to play a superbly gallant part in the defence of the city.

Brig. Pritam Singh deployed his garrison and set about organising a systematic defence. Picquets were posted on the surrounding hills in an iron ring and the men dug themselves into fox-holes in and around the city. Some of the picquets were as far as four miles from their headquarters but each was connected by a telephone line to the Brigade H. Q.

Local volunteers were trained and formed into militia units to assist the hard-pressed Indian and State battalions and while the defence was carried on, the officers and men of the garrison continued training themselves with evermore strenuous exercises. For example, a live grenade with the pin taken out would be dropped next to an officer; he had only four seconds in which to run to it, pick it up, throw it away and jump behind cover to save himself from being blown into as many small pieces as the grenade itself. Another exercise was in horseback riding. Every officer, whether he had ridden before or not, was made to ride wild ponies, bare-back, as a recreation. It was all part of a toughening-up process. The situation certainly demanded it. There was no place for laxity.

Some officers undergoing the grenade test for the first time would avoid picking it up and run instead for the trench, there to await the explosion. It sounded much more pleasant from behind cover. It was certainly safer. But sooner or later even those officers who to begin with had little confidence got used to this type of training in which danger played a major part. They responded to it more and more casually as the weeks passed by.

The defence of the city was not the only worry Brig. Pritam Singh had on his mind. The population had to be fed and there was little or no food available. Salt, so essential for health, had been in short supply throughout the State. At some places it could not be obtained at any price; even in Srinagar it was so scarce at this time that it cost Rs 20/- a seer—i.e. nearly £1 sterling for a pound in weight of salt. In Poonch city the problem was so acute that the alternatives were to eat without salt or go without food. Another problem was that of rickets, which quickly developed among the children as a result of lack of calcium.

Malnutrition was extremely prevalent amongst the refugees.

There were few who did not go hungry. The Army voluntarily gave up a large portion of its milk and other rations though they had to continue fighting in the bitterly cold wind on the frozen hilltops. Even cholera broke out at one time and a hasty sanitation drive had to be undertaken. In any case there were only two military doctors to attend to the aged and to the ever-increasing numbers of sick and under-nourished. These doctors worked themselves to the bone. Even births caused a problem for there were many mothers having babies and few people who knew how to attend to them. Why many of the babies did not die is a mystery; in the words of Major Suleman, "It was a matter of sheer pluck and good nursing after birth." In spite of the difficulties there were very few cases of mortality.

At one stage the stock of food was so depleted that the doctors went around preparing the people psychologically for the approaching crisis by teaching them that horseflesh was quite edible and not harmful. This would be available in quantity because of the many mules in the area. But when General Cariappa*, General Officer Commanding-in-Chief, Western Command, heard of this, he sent the following message immediately. "India has not reached that stage when her people must eat horseflesh; supplies will be sent; hold out."

But to make matters worse winter was approaching, bringing with it the severe Himalayan blizzards; and the men and women of Poonch were scantily clad. Many had nothing more than one thin cotton garment for they had with them only those things they could snatch in their hands in their panicky flight from their homes.

The Air-Strip

Nothing daunted Brig. Pritam Singh, who set to work constructing an air-strip with a determination characteristic of the Army. About 6,000 civilians joined hands with the troops, day and night, to complete the job. Wireless communication had by this

* Gen. K. M. Cariappa, O.B.E. later Commander-in-Chief of the Army.

time been established with the Base Headquarters and when the strip was ready a message was immediately sent over in code. So close was the air-strip to the hills that surrounded the city that a plane coming in to land could not approach direct. It had to circle downwards into the valley within the surrounding heights before wheeling in to land. And when taking off it had to go through a similar process swerving sharp to the right to avoid a hillside as soon as it was airborne, then climbing in slow monotonous circles until it had attained sufficient altitude to cross the mountain barrier and continue on its journey.

By 13 December pilots of the Indian Air Force took on the difficult task of landing a full section of mountain artillery at Poonch. The first to land was Air Commodore Mehar Singh, a man who cared little for hazards or dangers. Supplies now began to come in, but never fast enough to satisfy the appetites of the many thousands in the city, for the planes could not bring food alone—there was much military equipment, arms and ammunition to be brought and inevitably it was given a high priority. Besides, the weather was often unfavourable for the landing of planes which had frequently to be diverted with their loads to other parts of Kashmir. In due course, however, one more battalion of the Indian Army was flown in complete with its equipment.

"Operations Grain"

To augment the meagre food stocks, raids into enemy territory were organised. These were known as "Operations Grain". A force of troops—usually two or three companies reinforced by civilians whose job was to carry in the captured stocks—would venture out at dead of night and attack an enemy camp or village, throw the raiders into confusion and return home with whatever sacks of grain they could find. At times the people would even sally out to ripe wheat fields and harvest the grain themselves while our forces kept down the heads of the enemy snipers with well-directed fire. In this and similar ways the food stocks of Poonch were to a certain extent replenished.

One day during these operations the Commander was almost caught on the wrong foot. On such occasions it was a part of his policy to take with him as many officers and men as were available, leaving behind only a skeleton staff for defence—just enough men to hold the picquets against sporadic attacks. It was a gamble on the chance that while "Operations Grain" were in progress, there would be no concentrated attack from the enemy.

His Brigade Major (*ad hoc* and very temporary!) would leave Brigade Headquarters and lead a company of his own battalion in the operations whilst the Brigadier himself would go down to the status of a Regimental Commander by taking personal charge of one of the battalions and marching at its head—a fine soldier indeed. He was in front in many a bayonet charge.

If there happened to be two battalions going out in different directions, eventually to meet at a given rendezvous, he would still lead one of the two himself, only returning to his normal position as Brigade Commander to lead them both into action after they had joined forces. The Brigadier's main reason for taking a large force out of the city was to deceive the enemy who, seeing two battalions outside the perimeter, would naturally think that there was a larger force still inside, thus getting an impression that the defenders were numerically much stronger than they really were.

One day Brig. Pritam Singh had pushed a force about eight miles south into enemy territory when the hostiles chanced to attack Poonch in full force at night from the east. Our troops in the city held them at bay at the point of the bayonet, but the enemy kept persistently attacking in large numbers. A message was flashed to the Commander informing him of the situation and he and his force, wheeling swiftly round, fought its way back to Poonch by the shortest route, crossing hill and dale almost at the double for the full eight miles. Approaching the city at about four o'clock in the morning, the men silently took up positions on the picquets which were in danger. During their next attack the raiders' advance was met by a bayonet charge that was so fierce and unexpected that they were thrown back in panic and confusion to their original positions. It had been a narrow escape for the city but that thin ragged line had held until the main force returned.

Civilian Morale

Incidents such as this had to be taken in the defenders' stride and in this particular case it was not long before the Brigadier and his men went out once more. From the military point of view these patrols paid good dividends. By penetrating regularly into enemy territory the initiative was maintained even in defence. And as these operations into the surrounding country continued, the morale of the civilian population slowly but steadily improved. The enthusiastic band of followers began to regain confidence and to trust in the ability of the Army to hold out in spite of the odds against it.

But this had one unfortunate result. The civilian population of Poonch became less and less eager to flee to safer regions of Jammu. Planes which brought supplies to Poonch and were supposed to return to Jammu with refugees, did so with ever-decreasing numbers of passengers. On occasions they even took off empty. This added to our problems, for the bigger the population in the city the heavier the responsibilities and the greater the number of mouths to feed. Moreover, it was known that the enemy was reinforcing his troops and bringing up heavier guns. This was presenting the Commander with a problem that was more and more difficult to solve. Ultimately, instead of issuing permits to leave the city, he had to compel the people to go; and still they tried to stay.

The "Operations Grain", in which both men and women took part, aroused great enthusiasm and were carried out with a keen sense of anticipation, which was not without a touch of humour since a person was never able to tell just what quantity of grain he would bring back; sometimes it would be a full sack, at other times half and on occasions not even so much as a single grain. This element of chance seemed to keep the people's spirits high. It gave them something to gossip about and frequently enough it had its exciting moments. Often they would be found laying bets on the quantity of grain that could be obtained. A love of gambling lies deep in the hearts of these people and it could not be suppressed, however grim the circumstances. Actually such operations carried the highest stakes possible for in fact they were nothing less than a gamble in life itself. But since the work of collecting grain was a necessity it was done voluntarily and with pleasure. However hard the life in the city, most of the people preferred to put up with these perils rather than consider the dull existence they would otherwise be leading in a refugee camp in Jammu. It was their life and they lived it the only way they could in the circumstances—making the most of it. As Brig. Pritam Singh told me himself, whenever he asked a particular family to leave the mistress of the house would retort: "We will; but only when the Army does. Our homes are here and we do not intend to go until you do—and in any case we do not think you ever will."

"So," the Brigadier added, "how could we force them?"

Never a Step Back!

Winter set in, covering the country around with a white mantle of snow. Yet the enemy continued to attack. Sometimes they would make their onslaughts on a number of picquets at the same moment; at other times they would concentrate first on one hill and then on another; but whenever they came and however they attacked, they were always thrown back with losses, heavy at times. Valiantly our thin dogged line on those rugged hills of Poonch held on.

There was no going back, nay, not a foot! For one step in withdrawal one day and one more the next day would eventually amount to losing a hill and jeopardising the chances of survival of those within the city. So our men stood firm, grim and determined, with their bayonets fixed—a formidable and stern reminder to the enemy that we were there, and there to stay.

About the middle of March 1948 a gun duel commenced. The

enemy brought up their mountain artillery and bombarded the city, firing a number of shells in the civilian area; but it was the air-strip on which they concentrated and which suffered most of the damage. The garrison then started a counter-battery bombardment. We had guns of the same calibre as the enemy and each side went on shelling the other intensively. But the garrison was at a disadvantage for it was in an enclosed area while the enemy were free to move about, changing their positions. In addition the enemy were able to shell the air-strip whenever they expected a plane to land. While this did not necessarily cut our lifeline, it made the problem of getting supplies much greater and more hazardous.

The Garrison Commander asked for some longer range guns with which he could throw the enemy further back. At dusk one day four Dakotas loaded with 25-pounder guns took off from Jammu. While three of them flew at a high altitude one, piloted by Air Commodore Mehar Singh, flew dangerously low, hugging the valley and screening itself below the ridges until in reached Poonch. Then flying much lower than the heights surrounding the city, Mehar Singh landed to unload his guns unseen.

In the meantime the three remaining planes hovering high above Poonch gave the enemy the impression that they were the only aircraft in the vicinity. While flying around they made good use of their time by observing the positions of the enemy guns, which were very well camouflaged. When Mehar Singh signalled that he was ready to take off, having unloaded his guns, the other three planes came low over the city and circled around below the ridges without making any effort to land. Then one of the planes quietly detached itself from the trio and was immediately replaced by the Air Commodore's unloaded Dakota. Three planes again remained flying high above Poonch while the second Dakota, still unseen, landed and unloaded its guns.

By three such carefully timed switchovers all the guns were unloaded and the Dakotas flew home without the enemy having realised what had happened. It was a difficult task of airmanship and those pilots were worthy holders of the wings of their country. With the help of these 25-pounder guns the enemy was attacked west of Poonch city and forced to withdraw his artillery. In a short while the air-strip was again completely repaired and was ready for regular Dakota flights.

But though this gave some relief to the problem of getting supplies into Poonch, the enemy soon intensified his attacks and his ring around the city was slowly but steadily tightened.

4

General Thimayya Reorganises

A Signals Officer was required to organise communications in the Srinagar area under the command of Gen. Kulwant Singh, who was the General Officer Commanding, Jammu and Kashmir Area. Capt. P. S. Randhawa of 161 Brigade Signals was the only one there and his hands were full with the communications in the Uri sector. A few of his men were away in Poonch.

It is a well-known fact that when an army moves, it must move quickly and this particular instance was no exception to the rule. So it happened that even before I could collect my thoughts after receiving my orders, I found myself in a plane high above the Banihal Pass making for Kashmir. It was 12 April 1948 and I had come from Jammu. I was to organise communications in Srinagar and also to help in raising 163 Brigade Signal Section for the Brigade which was already in operations. This had to be completed before the mounting of the summer offensive. Second Lieutenant (now Captain) Gurdev Singh came a little later to complete the raising of this section.

Srinagar Signal Office

The Srinagar Signal Office was situated in a tiny room, little bigger than the small 20-line exchange which it contained. The adjoining one, which was about forty feet long and served as a guards' sleeping-room-cum-Signal Office was soon, on the General's orders, handed over solely for Signals' use. With only eight men I was confronted with the task of having to man four wireless links, the exchange and the Signal Office all 24 hours of the day, with lines to lay out and maintain as well as innumerable other duties. The prospects seemed anything but cheering, but I had reckoned without the unflinching devotion and unflagging capacity for endurance which my men proved to have.

In the absence of a senior non-commissioned officer to fill the very important and responsible appointment of Supervisor, Lance-Naik Promodh Singh and Signalmen Babu Ram and Bhan Singh together made it a point to see that this function was not neglected. They worked alternately on the exchange and the wireless sets after their eight-hour shifts of routine duties.

The trunk lines from the forward areas were linked via the civil exchange to the military exchange. This eased our work but unfortunately it also allowed a leakage of much secret information. We soon realised that the lines to Baramula, Uri and Bandipur—all operational areas—would have to be relaid and connected directly to the military exchange in order to ensure security.

Step by step our men got down to their task and our section became well organised, working day in and day out. A constant check had to be kept on wastage. Owing to our limited resources in personnel, batteries, petrol for charging and a shortage of equipment for replacement, our sets were put on scheduled timings. Wireless and Fullerphone* to Jammu were switched over alternately according to the classification of messages to be passed. Sometimes the weather took a hand, climatic conditions affecting either the lines or wireless in turn.

With all these teething troubles, it was a remarkable fact that there was never a query, an order or a message lost. The credit goes to those lads who put all they had and more into their tasks.

* Fullerphone—a line instrument for sending telegraph messages.

The Command is Divided

Not long after my arrival in Srinagar, Gen. Kulwant Singh left to take up his new appointment as Chief of the General Staff. The command was now divided into two—Jammu and Kashmir becoming separate areas. On 3 May 1948, General Thimayya who was General Officer-Commanding, Srinagar Division took over the Kashmir Area, which covered the whole of Kashmir Valley including Uri, Khargil and Leh and also Poonch for some time. The Zojila Pass between Srinagar and Leh was at this time in enemy hands. General Thimayya's formation was later called 19 Infantry Division.

Late in April, Gen. Atma Singh had been given command of the 2nd Airborne Division in the Jammu Area which included Rajauri, Naushera, Jhangar and later on Poonch. This formation was subsequently redesignated 26 Infantry Division.

The whole command, consisting of both Jammu and Kashmir Areas, was under Lieutenant General Cariappa, who was appointed General Officer Commanding-in-Chief, Western Command.

India had declared it her policy to use only her own nationals in this campaign. Accordingly, General Butcher, an Englishman who was then Commander-in-Chief of the Indian Army, did not visit Kashmir State after the operations had begun. The European civil pilots of the Indian National Airways piloting the Delhi–Srinagar service were also replaced by Indians.

The Prime Minister's Visit

The Prime Minister, Pandit Jawaharlal Nehru, was to visit Srinagar on Sunday, 9 May, 1948. A festival was to be held in his honour in the setting of the magnificent Dal Lake. I was given orders a few days before to hand over my commitments to 19 Divisional Signal Regiment and return to my original unit—26 (2 Airborne) Divisional Signals Regiment in the Jammu Area—but I planned to move after taking part in the festivities. Shortly before my transfer, however, General Thimayya decided to have his

The Prime Minister at Jammu with Gen. Atma Singh

The Prime Minister at the Festival in Srinagar

Gen. Kulwant Singh, Brigadier Sen and Brig. Harbaksh Singh engrossed in plans

General Thimayya, second from left, with G.O.C.-in-C. General Srinagesh and U.N.O. officials

Divisional Headquarters shifted to Baramula for, as he put it, to stay at Srinagar would have the psychological effect of making his Headquarters personnel static-minded. Accordingly Brig. B. S. Bhagat, Chief Signals Officer, Western Command who had come in from Delhi to tie up communications for the impending offensive, upset my plans for taking part in the festivities of 9 May and then leaving for Jammu, by ordering me to take the whole of Main Headquarters 19 Divisional Signal Regiment to Baramula to establish communications in advance.

Before I left General Thimayya gave me a complete picture of the situation and said, "You will complete your task in forty-eight hours and conform this personally. I shall not move until all communications are through." The fact that the General had realised the value of his signals communications and had got his Signals Officer in the picture personally and early was an asset and ensured one hundred per cent communications.

When we arrived at Baramula we got down to our task with resolution, cleaning and clearing up the area around. Having made a reconnaissance for the Divisional Signal Regiment, we set up a Signal Office and constructed a road leading in, bringing stones from several miles away. Sanitation was also taken in hand immediately with the aid of the medical authorities. Wells were disinfected and pools sprinkled with D.D.T. At the same time we laid lines, opened up the exchange and established eight wireless links. The work was completed in twenty-four hours. Besides having internal communications we were in contact with Delhi, Jammu, Pathankot, Uri, Skardu, Poonch and our forward picquets.

The situation was altogether different from any armed conflict we had taken part in before. For while we were engaged in active operations calling for the utmost efficiency we were only allowed equipment on the peace-time scale. This meant that there could be no wastage of any sort; everything such as petrol, rations, clothing and equipment had to be exactly accounted for. In spite of the actual operations we had to keep a complete check on every single item of materials and stores.

In World War II, there had been practically unlimited resources. Equipment was almost as easy to replace as the change of a currency note. Helpful though this was in the task of carrying on a total war, there is no doubt that it had encouraged a bad habit of wastefulness. But when we were fighting in Kashmir the equipment we were using was manufactured abroad and was difficult to obtain. To acquire it meant a heavy drain on the country's finances. It was, therefore, an active operation of a new kind requiring the highest of both war-and-peace-time standards. It was a new form of training in itself.

On 11th morning Brigadier Bhagat made a personal check-up of the Signal Office, the lines and the wireless links, probing into various installations, looking for weaknesses. He then reported to General Thimayya well within the forty-eight hours we had been given, that his communications were ready. In a few hours 19 Divisional Headquarters moved out of Srinagar and exactly a week later, on 18 May, the General launched the summer offensive.

Brig. L. P. Sen, D.S.O., who was in command of 161 Infantry Brigade, encountered Pakistani regular troops after advancing a short distance from Uri. There was fierce fighting and many deeds of valour were recorded on both sides. At the same time Brig. Harbaksh Singh, who was Officiating Commander of 163 Brig. (in place of Brigadier Katoch who had been slightly wounded in the leg earlier) made a swift right hook and literally raced through roadless country taking Kupwara, Tragham and Titwal where he halted to guard the long line of communications behind him. Over five thousand square miles of "hostile" territory were brought under our control, spreading panic and alarm amongst the enemy.

The Ladakh Valley

At the same time, General Thimayya had to consider the Ladakh Valley, which lay isolated far away to the north amidst the higher ranges of the Himalayas, practically inaccessible owing to its distant location and the absolute lack of roads from the main centre of military concentration in the Valley of Kashmir. Leh, in the Ladakh Valley, would probably have been lost to the enemy, but for the initiative used by General Thimayya at this juncture. A company of our own troops had marched the three hundred miles to Leh, arriving only shortly before a larger enemy force. Our troops now found themselves hard-pressed in the defence of the remote mountain capital and as their ammunition soon ran low, the Company Commander, believing that planes could not fly to Leh, gallantly sent a message saying that although the ammunition had almost been exhausted and was in urgent need of replacement, the Company would fight to the last man and the last round.

It was unfortunately also a belief in knowledgeable circles at Air Headquarters that it was not under any circumstances possible to supply the Leh garrison by air, since the Dakotas in Kashmir were not pressurised or equipped for high-altitude flying and were therefore not expected to fly above their normal maximum altitude of eleven thousand feet. The route to Leh meant climbing to twenty thousand feet or more.

General Thimayya was not convinced by the official arguments and was determined to get something done for his men in the mountain outpost. Late one night he went over to Group Captain Mehar Singh and placed before him the distressing situation which the Leh garrison was now in. After a short discussion he somehow managed to persuade the Group Captain to undertake the very great risk of flying himself and the General to Leh. The time fixed for the take-off was 5 a.m., hardly six hours after the discussion.

"When we arrived over Leh," the Group Captain told me later, "there was fighting going on and we were doubtful as to who was actually holding the place. But General Thimayya recognised his men and as we circled lower we knew that Leh was still in Indian hands. As we hovered over the mountain city, we knew we had already proved the possibility of Dakotas flying there with supplies and that we could drop the ammunition we had brought and return to Headquarters. But we also realised that it was as necessary for us actually to land there as to supply ammunition, since our landing personally would raise the men's spirits and provide them with an assurance of immense value in boosting up their morale.

"The situation looked so hopeless," continued the Group Captain, "that for a moment I was reluctant to attempt a landing. In the first place there was no air-strip and, secondly, the only level ground which we could see from the plane was not very far from where the fighting was going on. And, in addition, not only was I personally responsible for the Dakota, but also for the life of the General, which was naturally of the greatest concern to me. But General Thimayya, with his usual persuasive way, said, 'Look here, Mehar Singh; having come so far, can you leave those lads on their own? And surely if anyone can get down safely, it is you.'

"Well," went on the Group Captain, "if the Commander was willing to take the risk, it was hardly up to me to refuse. Of course the General is a damned good type! And so, looking around for a good spot, I landed on a dry river-bed without any mishap and took the precaution of keeping my engines running. Without delay a few of the lads gathered around us and began to unload the ammunition we had brought, whilst others levelled out some of the bumps on the ground in front of us as fast as they could."

Never in the history of Ladakh Valley had a plane landed or even flown over Leh. In view of the situation it was typical of the Commander of the Division, Gen. K. S. Thimayya, and the Commander of the Air Forces in the Kashmir Valley, that excellent and outstanding airman Group Captain, later Air Commodore, Mehar Singh, that this pair should have been the first to attempt this hazardous feat. The air route to Leh was now open and the garrison was in fact supplied in this manner throughout the campaign, with the result that the Valley of Ladakh remained in our hands.

Whilst these operations in the Kashmir Valley and in Ladakh were continuing at full pace, the number of words that passed and repassed through our Signal Office daily reached thirty, forty and sometimes fifty thousand. To cope with this huge task we had only two Junior Commissioned Officers and a hundred men at Baramula—twenty of the latter being linemen. A short while later, however, eight officers arrived almost together and all my responsibilities of the Main Headquarters Divisional Signals were handed over before I returned to my regiment in Jammu.

5

A Restless Month

THERE was trouble on the Jammu–Sialkot border. Sialkot is in Pakistan and not very far from India. Raids would take place at short intervals and the complaints that resulted usually went up the highest level in both countries—sometimes reaching the Prime Ministers. It was therefore decided by the Commanders-in-Chief of the Armies of India and Pakistan that all such border raids should be reported only to the lower formation commanders on the spot and left to them to sort out among themselves. A time was fixed for both Pakistani and Indian officers to meet on the border near Suchetgarh to discuss plans for putting an end to these hit-and-run tactics.

As a company commander in the Divisional Signal Regiment of the Jammu Area, I went down to inspect 268 Brigade Signal Section and for liaison with the Brigade staff. The Brigade Headquarters was then at Miransaheb, a few miles from the border on the Jammu side. The Brigade Commander took me and two others along with him to meet the Pakistani officers at the border conference. Each party was under the watchful eye of the respective forces, which were well hidden. After much handshaking and expressions of genuine pleasure at seeing each other, brothers-in-arms of the old days, we got down to work. Somehow our Brigadier had managed to convey a message earlier to the Pakistan Sub-Area Commander, an old friend of his, calling for a couple of bottles of whisky, which were brought along and duly paid for in Indian currency. This made the whole affair very friendly and there was a lot of laughter and chaffing of one another. We were soon talking about old times and acquaintances, though rather warily, and always cautious of the importance of security. My counterpart across the border was Maj. Mohammad Suleman of the Pakistan Signals. We had been subalterns together, had fought earlier in the same company in the Burma Campaign during World War II and were as friendly as brothers. Indeed he had once given me an English translation of the Koran to read and study.

We did not take long in settling the question for which we had assembled. We decided that the commanders on either side of the border should settle among themselves all disputes concerning raids within their respective territories and that no complaint should be allowed to go up to higher authority. We even laid plans to maintain a channel of communication on both wireless and line between the two opposing forces. Each was to run a telephone cable to the border where they would be joined together. The wavelength or frequency for the wireless link was also settled. Soon it was time for us to depart and we drank our last round "for the road" with a toast to everybody's health. Only I, since I do not drink, toasted our friends not in whisky but in lemon squash; my toast, however, was accepted just as genially as that of the others. Finally we departed.

Having laid our cable and opened up a wireless set, we waited the whole day for them to answer; but nothing happened. We held on for the second day, but there was no reply. Once again we waited, but still there was no communication.

By this time we became suspicious and, as we half expected, a raid was made two days later. But we were more than prepared and took a heavy toll of the attackers. After their rout they returned to security beyond the Pakistan border. Not much time had passed since we had been friends and brothers-in-arms, but now that seemed so long ago—and here we were in our positions on the opposite sides of the border, on the brink of an all-out conflict.

Poonch Waits Patiently

It was June 1948. After nearly eight months of siege the garrison in Poonch was still defending stoutly. Reconnaissance and fighting patrols were sent out in different directions as a matter of routine. "Operations Grain" still continued, though not with so much success as before, for the enemy had consolidated themselves to prevent the panic which our infiltrating tactics seemed to cause in the front areas.

However, our ability to take the initiative in defence continued as before. The people of Poonch went about their duties with no less fervour and with what looked like indifference to the dangers that surrounded them. The Parachute Kumaon Battalion, which had reached Poonch under Lt.Col. Pritam Singh in November 1947, was still there, always fighting in the thick of the battle. They had suffered casualties and much of their equipment had become worn out or damaged through continuous use and enemy action. It was now intended to pull this battalion out of the city for re-equipment and reorganisation.

In all sectors of Jammu and Kashmir more planes were required than before, for operations were extending and taking a sterner turn with our tentacles spreading into various areas which were under hostile control.

Since the few planes that we had at our service in those days were needed in so many places at the same time, it was not considered feasible to pull the garrison out of Poonch by air. There was also a possibility that what had so far been a localised conflict might, with very little provocation, develop into a major conflagration between the two countries. Indian Army reserves could not all be sent to Kashmir as another affair had loomed large on the Indian horizon—the affair of Hyderabad. At this very time this State, a pocket inside India, was becoming increasingly hostile. Under the rule of the Nizam those in power hoped to keep the state as a separate autocratic entity. This could hardly be tolerated. It was a festering sore requiring an operation—an operation which actually took place in July 1948 when the Indian Army took over control of the state.

A City of the Dead

Rajauri, a city of five thousand people, had been regained by the Indian forces earlier, in April. When our troops entered, headed by armoured columns, they were met by a deathlike silence in what appeared to be an abandoned city.

"Where are the people?" was the unasked question on everyone's lips. "Have they run away?"

The answer soon became painfully clear. We found it in the grotesque sight of dead and dying huddled in dark corners; men in heaps, women with the hair on their heads trembling in the breeze in mute appeal, and undernourished children. Some of the women had committed suicide by throwing themselves into wells rather than continue to suffer the ordeal they were undergoing. Cases were reported of young girls who were lucky enough to escape, more dead than alive, who had been assaulted by ten, twenty, thirty or more men. Others, we were told, had been dragged away screaming or unconscious.

However much one may be surprised at such terrible happenings, it must be remembered that the urge for retaliation and counter-retaliation amongst the civil population in those days was so powerful and so deeply rooted that such events must have been repeated frequently and in many places. There are no bonds that will hold fury backed by lust, hate and vengeance. Indeed the sights we saw told of massacre and cruelty that surpassed even that of Baramula. When we entered Rajauri we gazed on a grisly and sombre panorama—an abyss of crime.

No authority can guarantee a correct and exemplary behaviour of all its people. With the background of events such as were taking place in Kashmir, individuals with perverted mentalities, congenitally desirous of lust and revenge, may be expected to run amuck, and can be excused, however revolting their deeds. But to find evidence that hordes of people had stooped so low is beyond one's imagination.

In modern total warfare it is the women and children who have often to bear the brunt of the first onslaught—not the soldiers.

Such is war. But is not this all the more reason for the nations to make and keep a firm, solemn and abiding pact to leave women and children individually untouched, with stern reprisals for those who commit or encourage the beastly crime of mass rape? Such matters should not be taken for granted.

A Decision is Taken

The distance between Rajauri and Poonch via Mehndar is sixty miles. All the territory between these two places was occupied and fortified by the raiders. Mehndar itself, a town in the centre of the area and about thirty miles from each of the cities, had been turned into a strong enemy base headquarters and an important recruiting centre. Though this part of Jammu was infested with the enemy and strongly held, it was decided, in view of the shortage of planes, not to bring out the battalion from Poonch by air, but that an attempt should be made to battle to the city through these sixty difficult miles. Much of the route consisted of a continual series of spurs, keen-edged crags and crests rising to heights of 10,000 ft. and over, but we knew that if this deep and difficult penetration on foot into the heart of enemy fortified territory could be achieved it would serve a two-fold purpose. Firstly, the information obtained from what would be more or less a reconnaissance in force on the ground would in itself be invaluable for future operations. Secondly, there was the important psychological factor; the very audacity of the attempt to smash through the enemy fortifications over such a distance would have a severe and adverse effect on the morale of both the opposing forces and the half-million civilians living in the intermediate territory.

The repercussions were exactly as we had foreseen. The civil population had been instilled with much false propaganda disguised by the specious phraseology of the enemy, who made every effort to gain the assistance of the unthinking and easily duped masses in spreading far and wide the seeds of prejudice and terror. How close the people came to following the rattle of confused jargon till they realised for themselves its falsehoods, became very clear later. But suffice it to say that in the end truth did prevail, though it required much effort and patience in the proving.

6

The Break-Through

TO implement the decision to send a column to fight its way from Rajauri through the sixty miles of enemy territory to Poonch, a force was organised from the troops of 19 Infantry Brigade. The column was composed of the following:

1. A battalion of the Kumaon Rifles under Major Chand, Officiating Commanding Officer.
2. A battalion of the Punjab Regiment under Lt.Col. Jagjit Singh (there were two Punjab battalions in the area).
3. A Signal detachment of 19 Infantry Brigade Signal Company.
4. A Machine-gun Section (Madras).
5. A Mountain Battery (No. 5).
6. One squadron of 8 Animal Transport Regiment.
7. A detachment of 37 Assault Engineers.
8. An advanced Dressing Station.

This column was under the command of Lieutenant Colonel Dhillon, who was originally Commanding Officer of the Kumaon Rifles. His task was to reach Poonch, extricate the battalion of the Parachute Kumaons, and return with it to Rajauri.

A Signal detachment, which consisted of about twelve men, was put under Lt. Ram Singh, who was later wounded by the same shell which struck Brigadier Usman. In my position as Officer Commanding 3 Company in the (Airborne) Divisional Signals

Regiment, it was a part of my duties to keep in touch with Brigade Headquarters and the Brigade Signals Companies and Sections situated in the different sectors. I was therefore in direct touch with the Signal Section of Lieutenant Colonel Dhillon's column while it was engaged in operations.

A little later when the column was on the march I left for Poonch by air and asked the pilot to fly low to see if we could recognise our men. When we arrived at Poonch there were about eight bullet holes in the plane, two having just missed the petrol tank. It was good shooting.

The first objective was Thana Mandi, 15 miles from Rajauri. The route was towards the north-east, the place lying roughly east of Mehndar. It was proposed to capture and consolidate Thana Mandi and make it a firm base from which the column would push on.

The perimeter at Rajauri had a radius of no more than two miles. There was a broken road leading to Thana Mandi and along it were a number of villages inhabited by about twenty-five thousand civilians under enemy domination and amongst whom many raiders lived. There were hills 5500 ft. high on either side of the road leading through the Kallar defile. This defile was a position of strategic importance, about four miles short of Thana Mandi, and had to be captured in order to secure the road before making for the main objective. According to our plan, the capture was to be carried out by troops other than those of the column. These troops would form a protective armed gate for the column to pass through at the start of the operations.

A Stealthy Beginning

On the night of 14 June two companies set out—one from the Rajputana Rifles and the other from the second Punjab Battalion in the area.

The Punjabs moved along the river at the dead of night, unseen and undetected in spite of the fact that alongside the road there were many houses inhabited by the hostiles. The fast-flowing rivers

Regimental signallers leading

A wireless set on pack transport

Flying Officer

D. Barty

The muleteer taking supplies to picquets

Before the Beripattan Bridge was built

Berripattan Bridge being opened — a tribute to the Sapper

A Flying trolley

Crossing the river Munawwarwati

greatly helped the movement of these two companies by drowning the noise they made. They soon captured a height (Point 5,875) east of the pass and behind the enemy lines and then went on to take the defile completely by surprise.

Meanwhile the Rajputana Rifles, making an approach march by night, encountered opposition with mortar and gunfire shortly before reaching their own objective.

At dawn they launched their attack and, under support of the Artillery, pressed on and captured Maharajpur Ridge, an important position. Because of the shortage of troops it was not possible to picquet all the features along the route; many were left undefended, the troops having to content themselves with taking the risk of enemy infiltration by holding only a few strategic heights.

At 4 a.m. on the 15th the column set out for Thana Mandi on what was known as "Operation Gulab". It was accompanied by tanks and field guns to a little beyond Maharajpur, as far as the road was usable, but further on, near Siot, heavy, enemy automatic fire from nearby hills held up the column. A frontal attack was immediately made by the company of the Kumaonis, who dislodged the enemy after fierce fighting. These lads were in no mood to brook any delay in the early stages of the operation. Two more companies of the same regiment were sent forward west of the river to comb the hostiles out of the houses and to protect the left flank of the column against sniping.

The general advance was resumed at midday. The tanks and field guns were left behind but a battery of mountain guns were able to continue.

Brig. Yadunath Singh, 19 Brigade Commander, accompanied the column as far as Thana Mandi. There he conferred with the village headmen—the Nambardars. He assured them of our goodwill and offered any protection required. He made it clear that there was not the slightest intention to harm the civil population or cause them any intentional inconvenience. These men appeared convinced and overcome by his sincerity, and gradually all their oldest men who, as they said with considerable logic, "had nothing to lose but their lives, which were almost at an end". But when they saw that the old men felt satisfied, they sent their sons and other elders and ultimately, when they began to gain confidence and felt reassured that we did not intend to harm them, they came not only themselves, but with their wives, daughters and children. It was not long before the entire local population were convinced of the goodwill of the Brigadier and his small army of men who were offering them protection. In fact the people felt that the presence of an army was sufficient and that the necessity for further protection did not arise.

The first phase of "Operation Gulab" having been completed, the Brigadier returned to Rajauri, from there to advise and direct the column, if necessary, on its hazardous approach to Poonch. He was in close touch throughout by both wireless telegraphy and radio telephony. Incidentally, the Signals Junior Commissioned Officer accompanying the column was a young man called Jemadar Nair, who was later mentioned in despatches for the part he played in this operation.

The second phase opened with Lieutenant Colonel Dhillon and his men making a sudden thrust for Dheri-ki-Gali. The companies, always leap-frogging, one guarding the flanks while the other moved forward, took the place by surprise. They also had to capture two or three surrounding features before they could rest in order to ensure sufficient security to feed and water the mules. Though taking pack transport with them was a tedious task, the animals were invaluable for carrying supplies, mountain guns and ammunition; and though the enemy continued shelling our temporary picquets their needs were attended to.

The Pace Quickens

In due course the column set out again, quickening its pace though the going was very strenuous. Halting for rest was avoided except when it was inescapable, for the longer the column delayed the more time the enemy would have to form up and block their way or surround them.

When our men reached the village of Bafliaz they were gratified to see the whole population, all Muslims, turn out to greet them, offering sweets and milk which were accepted and given to the refugees they had released from the raiders and who had joined the column on its way. The villagers also surrendered the few women they had recovered from the raiders. This demonstration of friendliness encouraged us immensely, proving beyond doubt our own contention that the war was not one of religion but of principles. The people of these villages had shown their goodwill towards our men in spite of their being in the very heart of enemy territory. In fact, only a few hours before our arrival hostiles had been living among them, spreading false propaganda and disrupting their home life.

Meanwhile, Brig. Pritam Singh was instructed, as part of the coordinated relief plan, to advance the Parachute Kumaon Battalion from the Poonch perimeter so as to meet the column at a point twenty miles south of the city. After the join-up the combined formation was to attack the enemy stronghold at Mehndar, in order to destroy their recruiting centre. The column from Rajauri and the battalion from Poonch met at the village of Potha which lies south-east of the beleaguered city and north-east of Mehndar.

There were many friendly greetings, since the officers and men were all old friends. Though they had only been separated for a comparatively short period it seemed a long time since they had met, for much had happened in the meanwhile. When salutes and greetings were over, the job of evacuating the casualties which had been suffered on the march was taken in hand—some were badly wounded and were slowing the pace of others; besides, a number of weak and ailing refugees (including a few pregnant girls) had also tagged themselves on and had to be suitably provided for.

A Gallant Airman

An air-strip was hastily constructed. About 350 yds. long, it was just enough for an Auster or a Fairy Moth. We radioed for a plane and within a short time one was seen circling above. Even with so small a plane the pilot was reluctant to land for the strip was very small and appeared to lie close to a hill which had a clump of trees and a building on its crest. When eventually he did come down our men were most disappointed to learn that his small plane could only take away one casualty at a time. The delay was to our disadvantage.

Shortly afterwards a Dakota was seen circling overhead, but since our men knew that this type of plane required an air-strip about 1000 yds. long for landing they did not take any notice of it. After a short while it was seen to be circling lower and lower as though it was about to land. Somebody was heard to say: "No, it cannot be so! It is impossible, for the strip is too small. He'll kill himself, if he tries." Yet as these words were spoken, the plane began to straighten out and slow down in mid-air, seeming almost to hover. Then it descended on the strip, almost vertically, it appeared to make a perfect landing, though it just grazed the rough, raised ground at the far end where it frantically braked and turned round.

As soon as the plane stopped everyone rushed up to congratulate the pilot—Flying Officer D. Barty. But he warned everyone as he cautiously scanned the ground with those trees and the building on the hill, not to look so pleased for he had still to take off. Besides, if there was the slightest accident, notwithstanding the safe getaway of his passengers and himself, he could be court-martialled for having landed without orders and on his own initiative. This alone was a grave risk he was taking but, as he mentioned to me later, "I could not go away without landing, when I knew you lads seemed to be in an unpleasant position."

All the casualties and the refugees were emplaned and everyone waited breathlessly while the Dakota got into position for its take-off. The pilot warmed up his engines and at last made a start, taxying feverishly along the strip and just managing to persuade the heavy aircraft to leave the ground at the end of it. But alas! it looked as if he was heading straight for the hill. For a moment all thought that it was the end. Everyone held his breath. Then suddenly somehow that plane seemed to jerk upwards and miss those trees on the top of the hill by inches. To this day, it is difficult to imagine how that brave young pilot manoeuvred his plane as he did.

A week later in the Officers' Mess at Poonch, Maj. Gen. Atma Singh mentioned this incident. "I shall," he said, "get this pilot the worst rocket that can be given for taking that risk without orders." Then he added after a pause, "At the same time I shall recommend him for the highest award I can."

I remember these words of the General very distinctly and I remember him going at once and despatching a message to the Officer Commanding, Indian Air Force Wing.

Now that the wounded and the refugees had been taken away safely, we reinforced the column and, with Brig. Pritam Singh at its head, left Potha with a much lighter step. Four miles from Mehndar the enemy were entrenched in force. They were swiftly attacked and taken by surprise and after a short, stiff encounter, in which our artillery also played a part, enemy resistance crumbled and soldiers in thousands were seen running with the civilian population in all directions.

The civilians in this area were practically all armed and were used as auxiliaries by the raiders; but our attack completely demoralised them and, with the Punjabs now as an advance guard, the column entered Mehndar at 10 a.m. on 20 June. The enemy had had no opportunity to effect his customary scorched-earth policy, since he had been caught completely unawares. He had not even dreamed that the column would wheel south-west from Potha and make so daring an attack on his fortress, instead of going straight on to the comparative security of Poonch.

On to Poonch

Time was always a factor to be reckoned with. With hostile territory on all sides, the column had now to get out safely before the enemy could reorganise his forces. Having completed its task at Mehndar, its main object had still to be achieved—that of reaching Poonch. The column therefore formed up and moved out as soon as it was dark.

Our men had now been on the march for five days on field-scale rations and *shakarpara* (Indian biscuits), only on one or two occasions having had a cooked meal. The morale of the men was high and they were in fine fettle, fighting fit and eager to smash any enemy that stood before them. Even the youngsters in our force now felt they were veterans.

The column was held up by heavy machine-gun fire from Thopa Ridge, about ten miles north of Mehndar. While a frontal assault was being made on the ridge by the Parachute Kumaons, the Punjab Battalion swiftly circled round the enemy position and attacked them from behind. The hostiles fled leaving many of their men dead. The Kumaon Rifles (a different battalion from the Parachute Kumaons), not to be outdone, took possession of the surrounding hills. In this way, continually fighting, with units leap-frogging one another and with perfect team-work, the column wended its way forward, tired but full of fight, and soon arrived within sight of Poonch. Then quickly and with justifiable satisfaction it entered the perimeter under the watchful eyes of our sentinels high up on the mountain tops.

One part of the task was completed but the more hazardous part had yet to be done. The enemy had been alerted throughout the area and were now waiting and watching in the hope of destroying those who would be returning to Rajauri.

I was at Poonch when the column arrived. The ovation given to the *jawans* will long be remembered. The whole population—men, women and children—lined up to greet them, cheering and waving them in. These were the hardy men of Poonch and their beautiful, full-blossomed women who, a few months earlier, had been through the rigours of the winter scantily clad and poorly fed. But today, 22 June 1948, the womenfolk had come dressed in multifarious shades, adding a rich profusion of colour to the picturesque background of the Himalayan landscape. And with their lilting music and melodious singing they added a touch of personal charm and loveliness to the occasion as they swayed to and fro in rhythmic motion, shyly but coquettishly showering flowers on the soldiers.

What a wonderful welcome! Well had it been deserved. Before it started this operation had been named "Gulab" which means roses. Yes, it was a happy coincidence for we were now surrounded by the roses of Poonch.

Family Reunion

The arrival of the column in Poonch meant that a number of refugees who had come along with us had now reached their homes. To one family, for instance, we returned two young men and a girl. The girl Sita went back to her husband. She was welcomed with open arms. Her brother Mohan Lal returned to his parents along with his brother-in-law, whose wife had given him up for dead. Being all of one family, it was obviously an occasion for great rejoicing. Seldom can a household have had greater cause for joy, yet the moment the members of the family met their lost ones it seemed so incredible to them that they were alive that all they could do was to burst into tears and weep their hearts out. That night their was neither rejoicing nor laughter in their small house, where a light burnt all the night through. The silent hours of darkness were spent in prayer and meditation. This was the way which the family chose to offer thanksgiving to the Hand of Providence which had guided back to them their two sons and a daughter.

Next morning at a ceremonial parade, Maj. Gen. Atma Singh, Commander of the Jammu Division, took the salute. The officers and men of the column, spick and span, had turned out as smartly as though they had been in a peace-time station. Their stout hearts and heads were held high and within them was a feeling of pride.

When the message was radioed "Objective achieved, troops arrived in Poonch," a thrill went through all our forces in Jammu and Kashmir. It proved to all that the confidence they had in their own ability, the officers in their men and the men in their officers, in their courage and resourcefulness and in the ability of their leadership, was justified. Our arrival in Poonch acted as a tonic and boosted the morale of the entire Indian forces in Kashmir. The risk had been well worth taking.

Furthermore the column, forcing and fighting its way from Rajauri through sixty miles of enemy-infested territory, had shaken the morale of the enemy over an area of a thousand square miles, leaving him dazed and doubting his own ability to fight. His training and recruiting centre at Mehndar had been completely destroyed. In fact, when all is taken into consideration, one realises that our lads had unknowingly achieved much more than their official objective; and it had been well done.

I had been flown to Poonch from Jammu to reorganise the Poonch Brigade communications. It did not take long for me to convince the Brigadier that a good place was needed for the Signal Office; and at once he allotted an outhouse of Moti Mahal Palace. There I set to work and decided what new equipment and personnel were necessary. Both would have to be obtained from the Divisional Signal Regiment at Jammu.

Second Lieutenant Gurdev Singh, who had been with me in Srinagar raising 163 Brigade Signals Section, now came to Poonch and was left in charge of the Section there. He was a very busy man, for Poonch Brigade Headquarters was so short of staff that he was not only Signals Officer, but also Camp Commandant and at times Staff Captain as well. In fact, I believe one day he worked as Signals Officer-cum-Brigade Major! Though he proved equal to his duties, such multiple appointments should be discouraged, for when a Signals Officer has to do various jobs other than his legitimate signals work it can very easily have an adverse effect on communications. In these circumstances, however, it was fitting that 2/Lt. Gurdev Singh received a well-earned Mention in Despatches for the part he played in Poonch.

Back to Headquarters

For full seven days the men rested; they had no picquet duties nor did they take part in minor operations. But their physical training continued as usual at 6 o'clock every morning, after which they spent about three hours in cleaning, maintaining and testing their arms and equipment. After this they spent another two hours in normal fitness training, running up and down hills in full equipment. After midday there was not much else for them to do apart from their own internal unit guard and other routine duties. They would spend the afternoons resting, with games in the evening and the daily conference at which every man was given the latest details of the general situation.

The day at last approached when they had to return to their own headquarters—19 Infantry Brigade at Rajauri. On 29 June, the Poonch Brigade made a sortie towards Bhag and Salotri to confuse the enemy, and on the following day at 6 p.m. the column left the city and marched out into enemy territory to fend for itself. Its composition was the same as before except that it had been joined by the Parachute Kumaons, who were returning to Rajauri for reorganisation and re-equipment.

By a forced march Mehndar was reached on 1 July and from there the column immediately pushed forward at great speed towards Bhimbar Gali, only twenty miles short of Rajauri. But the enemy, who had shown signs of disorganisation at the beginning of this return journey, had by now concentrated in force on all the dominating heights between the column and Rajauri. He had regrouped in full strength, bringing in every available hostiles from an area of over a hundred square miles around. He had thus established a firm line, though his men coerced by propaganda and threats of punishment.

Both sides manoeuvred for position with an exchange of mortar and artillery fire. From the clatter and shouting that we could hear it appeared that the enemy was preparing to make an attack. In actual fact, as we learnt later, he had already had such a severe trouncing at the hands of the same column on its way to Poonch that his spirit was lacking. He was to all intents and purposes reluctant to come to a conclusion.

It was thus that the opposing forces were poised facing one another. Our men were only eighteen miles from "home" and their waiting comrades—so near and yet so far. Messages flashed between the column and its headquarters in the city. Our

Commander wanted to avoid a head-on clash for there would be no element of surprise were he to attack. Companies of the Rajputana Rifles and the Punjab and Jat Regiments which had assisted by forming a defile at the start of "Operation Gulab" were standing by; at once they moved out of Rajauri. Their task was to fight their way towards Makot and establish a line of defended hills for the column to march through. But soon after leaving the city on their properly named "Operation Hail", they came up against a heavy concentration of the enemy and, meeting, stiff resistance, they quickly diverted westward towards Kunial-di-Gali. There, catching the enemy unawares, they captured the hill and other surrounding heights, informing both 19 Brigade Headquarters and the column of the situation.

Having established their outposts well inside enemy territory, they naturally came under continuous mortar fire and sniping, but they held out and sent regular patrols to reconnoitre. Brigade Headquarters signalled Lieutenant Colonel Dhillon and his lads to meet one of the patrols at a given rendezvous. In the pitch-black darkness of the night the column and the patrol started from their respective places, following instructions closely. The patrol contacted the column at the chosen spot and quietly led it back within the protective range of our own guns. Our men were soon under the friendly eyes of our own troops on the hilltops of the newly formed armed cordon at Kunial-di-Gali, completely baffling the enemy, who were still waiting for an attack south of Bhimbar Gali and were still hesitating whether to attack first.

From Kunial-di-Gali our plucky lads made their way back to Rajauri—it was "Operation Hail" in all respects—a quiet *shabash* and a very *bara khana* (a grand lunch or dinner)—and then to rest, the need of the moment. Oblivious of everything else, they resigned themselves to sleep while others watched. It was a pleasant change to be given a day's complete rest, which meant no operations, no duties and no toughening-up exercises—but then the whole operation had itself been a toughening exercise of the most exacting kind. And the lads rested with a sense of deep satisfaction—a justifiable contentment that men in all modesty feel when a great work has been done and done well.

Yes, they had earned their respite and no one could deny them the right to a little rest. For a small force to penetrate into enemy-controlled territory to so great a depth and return safely, when the foe was ready and waiting to trap them was truly a fine achievement. Leadership of the highest quality, resourcefulness, imagination and forethought had not been found lacking in the young officers who took part. They had indeed shown their ability to be a step ahead of the enemy. And the *jawans*, right down to that great-hearted man the muleteer, had shown enthusiasm, courage and a quiet confidence in their own ability. There had been no fuss, no fluster. The job had been done with a quiet assurance.

There is no need to say more. The achievement of the task itself was sufficient proof of the quality of the men of the Indian Army—the salt of the nation.

7

Interim Period—July to September

IN July I was posted to 19 Infantry Brigade Signal Company which had its headquarters at Naushera. For once 13 was not an unlucky number; there were 13 battalions under the Brigade Headquarters, four times the number that a Brigade Headquarters is theoretically capable of coping with. The area it was operating in covered a part of the mountain ranges opposite Seri, from Sunderbani to Beripattan and also through Chingas to Rajauri.

With Brigadier Yadunath Singh

The Commander was Brig. (now Major General) Yadunath Singh. He was a teetotaller, a vegetarian and a non-smoker. His great powers of endurance are fully illustrated by an incident which I remember. During the monsoon we had completed a short operation at two o'clock in the morning. This was followed by a conference and we were to be ready again by 5 a.m.

He advised us to get some rest, which we did behind cover with the sky as our roof, as our positions were being subjected to mortar fire and it was safer in the open. I woke up suddenly with a start. I could not believe what I saw. The first thought that struck me was: "Here is the abominable snow-man upon us for our sins! Or is it just the enemy creeping up slowly?" But no, I suddenly realised with a deep sigh of relief that it was only the Brigadier saying his prayers at half past three, making a ghostly silhouette against the sky. There he was, sitting cross-legged, straight of posture, with his hands stretched out on his knees, lost in thought as though in a trance. Was this his way of getting physical and mental repose? I could not say. But it was a part of his routine to pray for four hours a day—two hours in the morning and again two in the evening—a routine he strictly adhered to even in the battlefield. By profession this great man was a soldier and one of marked military disposition; the Army was his chosen career. Yet in Kashmir today he appeared to be at heart a "Rishi" inclined towards a deeply religious life. Right in the midst of the operations he would find time to lose himself in long moments of deep meditation.

The Commander paid frequent visits to his troops, knowing full well the value of keeping in touch with his men, particularly those in the thick of things or on lonely picquets. He would often sit with them talking and exchanging views in a spirit of comeraderie. One day he organised a *bara khana* for both officers and men. Under his instructions the food was cooked by the sweepers and was served by the sweepers only. It was very good and enjoyed by all!

Like the Brigadier, Gen. Atma Singh also often used to visit our far-flung picquets to talk to the men. Neither did the G.O.C.-in-C., Lieutenant General Cariappa, ever miss an opportunity to have a chat with his *jawans*; nor Lieutenant General Srinagesh when he took over. These high-ranking officers came in spite of their preoccupation with multitudinous problems of high priority. They proved over and over again that in an officer, ability to mingle with his men on the basis of equality and understanding is as important as any degree of technical and tactical skill.

19 Brigade Signals

The Signal Unit of this Brigade was to provide and maintain communications with thirteen battalions, a task which is normally done by three Brigade Signals Sections. But these were not normal times—not in Jammu and Kashmir. The equipment, meant to serve three or at the most four battalions, had somehow to be stretched to make an efficient signals network for thirteen for, on account of long and slender lines of communications, additional apparatus could not be brought in fast enough.

The shortage of equipment was not our only difficulty. It was not at all easy to procure skilled operators and linemen, for the Divisional Signal Regiment was fully occupied and was much below its normal strength. Since we were short of operators only two were put on the wireless sets in the battalion instead of the usual three. Each man had to stay alert for twelve hours a day. After that, in addition to their own work on the sets or in the Signal Office, the operators were always required for various other small duties. As far as rest was concerned one day was as good as another. Saturdays and Sundays were like any other days in the week, and sometimes passed without our ever being aware of them.

In general a brigade seldom has more than thirteen miles of cable to lay and maintain, but in our case ten linemen had to lay and look after approximately one hundred and fifty miles of cable. To keep these lines in order was a major task as some of them stretched for forty miles while in theory the voice on a telephone should be clearly audible only for ten to fifteen miles. As a result, conversation from the opposite ends of the longer lines was often almost inaudible and sometimes had to be cut into pieces, the last two or three words being shouted in a high pitch at the top of one's voice. The person at the receiving end would have to reconstruct the message as well as he could and reply accordingly.

This, however, was good practice for radio telephony which requires the same manner of emphasis on particular words. Similar was the case with the special high-powered telephones which were utilised when available. At the end of each piece of conversation, the operator had to say "over", which means "your turn to speak". One General, as a test, used a long-distance telephone for the first time to ring up his wife in Delhi. Since she was not accustomed to hearing "over" she got more and more annoyed as the General kept repeating it until at last she flew into a temper pulling him up for saying "over"—Over what? The confusion was clarified by express correspondence from the General himself!

A factor that gave much trouble was the damage to the lines caused by sniping and mortar fire. But the linemen under Havildar Narayan, whose name became synonymous with lines in the Brigade, worked day and night to keep them in order. Whenever the Hávildar and his men set out to locate and repair a fault, they took along some camouflage nets and improvised fishing devices as part of their equipment. As there was always at least one river to cross, they would invariably get permission to bathe after finishing their task and they never failed to come back with sacks of fish sufficient for breakfast, lunch and dinner and with sometimes enough even to distribute to Brigade Headquarters Units. To all it was a welcome change from the usual rations.

Roads and Transport

As there were few bridges, trucks had to be ferried and many got held up—sometimes fifty or sixty at a time. In the earlier days men were thus caught, often in rain or snow with slush and mud on all sides. They would have to wait there with their trucks in the open taking the full force of biting cold winds of hurricane intensity, with rain often driving almost horizontally—and all this at altitudes of many thousands of feet.

With the absence of good roads and with only tracks which were hardly even visible, the Royal Indian Army Supply Corps, as it was then known, had an unenviable task which the extreme weather conditions made even more difficult. Supplies had to be taken to far-flung parts of the mountainous country, which meant days of marching. Reserves had to be stocked almost everywhere, in case of unforeseen eventualities, and supplies invariably had to be sent to reach their destinations much in advance of the actual operations.

Material, arms and ammunition had to be transported in various ways—by plane; by parachute; by road transport: ranging from ten-tonners to jeeps running on roads that were treacherous as a result of heavy rains and landslides; and by animal transport and porters to hitherto unapproachable place where mules had sometimes to jump from one ledge to another, occasionally missing their foothold and being hurtled to death hundreds of feet below. These men and animals of the Supply and Transport Services faced fierce blizzards and cold biting winds in semi-Arctic conditions, 30 degrees below zero when even mules—those hardy animals—can freeze to death. War is a heavy consumer of all the main essentials of life—requiring almost seven times the needs of normal day-to-day living. And it was the Supply men who had to keep up a continuous stream of these vital necessities of life.

By the middle of 1948, the lines of communications were becoming well organised. The heads of all branches of the Army had planned, devised, organised and coordinated schemes. Minute calculations were being made by our staff officers with exact timings which would be put into operation with precision. There was system and method in this work and it was due in no small measure to the keen supervision and immense drive of General Cariappa.

Many small bridges were springing up like mushrooms over a wide area. Where our main lines of communications entered from India, which supplied the life-blood to our forces, the Engineers were completing major bridges which had been constructed at immense speed against the coming rains. The Madras, the Bombay and the Bengal Sappers and Miners, all tried men, carried out their task most efficiently. Bridges over the Ravi, Uri and Basanter rivers, each with a span of more than 150 ft. were constructed in a matter of months. Among remarkable construction was the Bailey suspension bridge erected over the river at Beripattan. It linked Naushera, Jhangar and Rajauri and other places with Jammu.

The bridge across the Ravi was opened by the Indian Prime Minister himself; the Uri bridge by the General and the Basanter bridge by a State Minister. But the honour of opening the bridge at Beripattan was given to two Sappers, Namdev Power and Tula Ram—both men of the lowest skilled rank in the Engineers. Lieutenant General Cariappa said that the way this bridge had been constructed had given the Army a lesson in unity and cooperation. "To work like a team is the motto of the Army of free India. I would like to congratulate you on the fine piece of work that has been done in building this bridge."

Another branch of the Army that deserves great praise for the work done in Kashmir was the Medical Corps. We were extremely short of doctors and they had an immense amount of difficult work to do, serving not only our men but often the civilian population too.

The Unknown Doctor

I remember one occasion when an untiring doctor acquired the reputation of a god among the people of a certain village. I was on the east side of one of the small rivers which crossed the road between Beripattan and Naushera. I saw a young civilian of about 24 years, over six feet tall, lithe and straight of features, with a small child perched on his shoulder about to cross the fast-rising stream, much against the advice of his friends. With expressive gestures he was assuring everyone that he knew the shallows of the crossing for, said he, he had crossed this river many times before. And he certainly did not feel like waiting in the rain, possibly for the whole night, until the river subsided. His wife and parents were on the other side and the place was not far from his village.

Without more delay he waded in and was halfway across when the villagers on the other bank began telling him to hurry. The stream was rising so fast that the water level had gone up a foot since he had begun the crossing, and was now almost five feet deep at the centre. When he heard his friends calling, the man suddenly faltered. He looked around nervously and appeared to be wondering whether to continue or to return. But pulling himself together, he went on steadily step by step. When he had almost reached the opposite bank and had already passed the child into safe and eager hands, he suddenly lost his balance and was swept away downstream by the swift current. He did not know how to swim.

As the bank jutted out on both sides, there was a possibility that his body might be washed away under the overhanging portion. The wails of men and women, helpless spectators of this incident, rent the air. The women beat their bosoms, tore their clothes and flung themselves on the ground. Their cries aroused the nearby villagers and brought them hastily to the scene, where two of his friends immediately dived into the water to try to rescue him. We at the far bank looked on helplessly at the spectacle.

About five minutes must have elapsed before the body was recovered from the angry waters. By one of those rare coincidences, an Army doctor, a Captain, happened to arrive at that very moment at the opposite bank of the river looking for a place to cross. Immediately he rendered first aid to the lifeless body, while the women's wailing died down to a low moan of doubt and fear.

Turning the man on his stomach, the doctor forced gallons of water out of him and began massaging and slapping him so fiercely that we could hear the resounding slaps from where we were across the raging river. He twisted and shook the man's limbs as though the poor fellow was a contortionist. Had he been conscious, he would no doubt have protested loudly at being so roughly handled.

This display of wrestling continued for over an hour while we watched and wondered why the doctor kept at it with such perseverance and energy, when there seemed to be no hope. His efforts seemed nothing more than a fine, but useless, manifestation of his mission to save life.

We were almost losing interest when the moans on the far bank suddenly gave way to loud yells. We wondered what had happened, but soon realised that the cries were cries of joy for the man had moved his head of his own accord after more than an hour of massaging and artificial respiration. He was alive again and it was only a matter of a few minutes more before he was brought fully back to consciousness and was able to stand on his feet. Then, while the relatives were clinging to him and showering blessings on him, the doctor quietly slipped away. As far as he was concerned, he had done his task. There was nothing more for him to wait for.

Had that doctor not been guided by the hand of Fate to that particular spot, the young man would have certainly died, for his relatives stunned by what they had seen, had already given him up for dead. While the doctor was continuing with his untiring efforts to do anything that was humanly possible to bring the spark of life back into the lifeless body, they had looked askance at one another with a feeling of doubt and even suspicion. But the following day, when we were able to cross the river, we discovered that no one knew the name or the whereabouts of the doctor. I searched for that doctor for a long time only for one reason—to shake hands with him—but I never found him. The story is therefore not the story of one single man, but a tribute to all those who attended the sick in Kashmir. Today the river where this incident took place has been bridged high over the water; the bridge stands as a tribute to that nameless doctor.

TRAINING

The most conspicuous development in the training of our men was perhaps the increased battle skill and improved field-and-jungle craft they acquired, and the constant reorganisation of training methods as the Army devised new and better means of tackling its problems. Fortified by battle experience and encouraged by higher appreciation of the value of sound training, a strenuous physical, psychological and technical programme of training was put in hand. Drill continued. Discipline was strict. The necessity of a very high standard of physical fitness, to condition both officers and men to the rigours of hill-climbing at a fast pace was fully appreciated. This fitness training, which entailed men of all ranks running up and down hills for long periods in full equipment, was never relaxed. I remember seeing, amongst many others, an officer—Capt. D. Gear—who never ventured out without his full pack, equipment, arms and water bottle, even when visiting his friends at the neighbouring Officers' Mess, three or four miles away. Shouldering the extra twenty pounds of weight became as much of a routine to him as the wearing of his boots. And the ability to do so at all times was only achieved by constant practice.

To develop mental alertness, self-confidence and ability to make on-the-spot decisions, mock battles and TEWTS (Tactical Exercises without Troops—done on a sand-table replica of the terrain under operation) were held frequently under the supervision of the local commanders, Brig. Yadunath Singh and Gen. Atma Singh. Flexibility of mind was of paramount importance. Fluidity of thought and ability to alter pre-arranged plans at short notice in order to meet the quickly changing situation and unexpected developments which continually arose, were developed by regular exercises, schemes and small night and day operations. Fortunately military training in itself tends to stimulate quickness of thought, a fact that became clearly visible in the extreme mental and physical alertness of the personnel in the Kashmir area.

Courses and lectures by specialists were organised throughout the area itself for officers and men. Education for other ranks was compulsory. And as time passed, the ability for improvisation was steadily reaching such a high standard that the improvised product itself was often as ingenious and effective as the original.

While this training continued there was no respite in the enemy sniping and machine gunning. All the while our troops had continually to probe the enemy defences in order to maintain the initiative which we indeed held throughout.

It was in the midst of this training period, in September 1948, that we heard the news that the Hyderabad Police Action, had been successfully concluded. Before this the Hyderabad question had required the holding of Indian troops in various places to stamp out any fifth-columnist risings. The end of it had, as expected, relieved pressure on the troops everywhere, for this action was the culmination of the Government of India's policy to bring over five hundred states within the borders of the country into the Union of India. It was an event that indirectly gave new strength to our men in Kashmir.

The Army as Administrator

By this time 19 Infantry Brigade had over half a million civilians under its jurisdiction. About 450,000 of them were Muslims, most of whom had come back to their homes from across the border after our advance. The truth about the fair treatment given by the Indian forces to all, irrespective of religion, spread not only throughout the State but across the Pakistan border in spite of the enemy's adverse propaganda. Whole families came back to their homes in thousands, not suspiciously as before—the men first and the womenfolk after.

Overnight the Army had taken over the task of administration, providing assistance and supplying necessities to the civil population. Inconspicuously and unassumingly our soldiers began to look after the people with care and tenderness as though they were their own kith and kin—a rôle which had not been thought possible for men in uniform to carry out, but which they conducted with a high sense of responsibility tempered with human and rational judgment. These men, trained under normal conditions only for their primary task of waging war, now showed their remarkable versatility and ability to take up the responsibilities of guardians of a people whose main desire was to live at peace and in liberty.

Before very long the Army had to fight two battles as "Errands of Mercy". One was for the relief of Leh. This entailed the capture of the Zojila Pass, 11,500 ft. high. It was a battle as colourful and vivid as any in the history of the country—but that is another story.

The other was the final relief of Poonch. Unlike the first operation, which was only a temporary break-through, the object of the second was to throw the enemy right back and to capture and hold a wide expanse of territory in order to ensure a safe passage for food supplies and other essential materials by a permanent overland route connecting Rajauri with Poonch and the surrounding districts.

With the coordination of the various branches of the services now brought to as perfect a state as possible and with the growing experience the Air Force had acquired of operating in mountain country, the Indian Army in Kashmir had reorganised itself into a well-knit and first-class fighting and administrative machine suited to the area in which it was operating. Indeed it was proud to know it had reached this high standard of efficiency when officered in the operational theatre for the first time by Indians only.

It had developed a new *Esprit de corps* and a sense of teamwork seldom visible in days gone by. Officers and men of diverse religions and tongues, castes and creeds, had learnt to put into practice the principles of democratic and secular way of life and to live up to the high standards of efficiency and the colourful age-old traditions that it took over from its predecessors. Each man individually contributed his own share—no one less or more than the other—towards the same end, the Army.

The success of all these changes was due in no small measure to the top leadership directed by Gen. K. M. Cariappa, who was later destined to guide the future of the whole Indian Army as its first Indian Commander-in-Chief. But he could not have achieved this great work alone and it was the cooperation and drive of his generals and other officers, and the discipline and loyalty of the men, that helped him complete the task so smoothly and successfully.

8

Preliminary Blows

POONCH was now becoming both militarily and politically a thorn in the side of the enemy. Potentially it was a very important centre from which roads led in all directions. Though isolated in the midst of enemy territory, it provided a formidable and constant menace to his lines of communications. It cut off his forces at Chakoti and Haji Pir Pass in the north, from his southern bastions at Mehndar and Kotli, and was a formidable bridgehead in our hands against any attack on the Kashmir Valley, Baramula or Srinagar. Had his forces joined it would have more than doubled his attacking power. From the enemy's point of view there were possible approaches leading to Poonch from Rawalpindi, Jhelum and Murree in Pakistan.

Our continued defence of Poonch greatly reduced the value of the enemy's propaganda, and his promise to take possession of the whole of Kashmir could not have much force so long as our small garrison held fast in the city against numerically superior odds. Our staying in the city also had an adverse effect on the morale in the enemy camp since a considerable number of his troops were Poonchis, who had deserted from the city in the early stages, while many more were inhabitants of the countryside around.

Feeling that it was high time he obtained some spectacular

results, the enemy decided to launch concentrated attacks on one of the Poonch picquets intending to crash through by sheer weight of numbers and fire power, and so smash open the way for the rest of his forces to enter the city.

He brought up all the guns he could muster in the area—his 6-pound tank-blasters, which fire a direct trajectory, to smash through bunker slits and provide a close-range high-velocity blast, his mountain guns, 3.7 inch howitzers and his 25-pounders with some 4.2 inch mortars. He then blasted the ridge in an attempt to destroy the bunkers, first with one set of guns and then with mortars, and finally with the concentrated barrage of guns and mortars together.

When he suddenly stopped firing, leaving the hill smoking and smouldering, he advanced under the impression that nothing could have survived that shelling. Nevertheless he moved forward warily, almost a thousand strong, under the protection of his own machine-gun fire for he was fully aware of the calibre of the men he had to deal with.

When close enough he charged, but not one step did we give. He charged and charged again, but we were always there with our bayonets fixed throwing him back with heavy casualties. He then threw in fresh troops—about another thousand. They flung themselves at us again and again but still we withstood their attack. Though we were a handful, a mere hundred, we did not budge an inch.

Then at the psychological moment when the attack was weakening, our men who had been patiently restraining themselves in spite of their anger, burst out of their bunkers and with one terrifying battle cry flung themselves at the enemy bayoneting him into confusion and chasing him right out of close gun-range to lick his wounds, wherever he liked and so long as he was out of our sight. It was thus that those enemy battalions were repulsed and the fangs of their attack blunted. Never again did the hostiles attempt a frontal attack. That last attempt was in September 1948—an eventful month indeed.

A Land Link Necessary

Since the onslaught had failed the enemy evidently decided to attempt to starve the garrison into submission. He intensified the ring around the city and brought up his 25-pounder guns. He had every nook and corner of the city registered and he pounded the aerodrome regularly. Since all routes to Poonch were still cut its supplies and maintenance stores had to be brought by air; but with the aerodrome being constantly damaged by shell fire the Dakotas carrying these supplies could no longer land in safety with the result that there were only ten days' supplies left. At the same time the enemy made it difficult even for planes to come low enough to drop anything from the air.

Simultaneously the enemy was building up his forces at Bhag, a town only fifteen miles north-west of Poonch. This place was only twenty miles from the Pakistan border with which it was connected by a good road. It was therefore easy for him to build it up as a base from which to reinforce his troops around Poonch, for a still larger and final onslaught on the city, when he considered his starvation policy had had a sufficiently weakening effect.

From our point of view the situation was certainly deteriorating and demanded immediate action on our part. There were still ten thousand human beings in the city whose safety was of primary importance. Winter was fast approaching and with it many hardships were on their way. Besides, from a military point of view the weather would also be a serious handicap to mobility—one of our important weapons. It was therefore soon realised at all levels of Command that the immediate establishment of a land supply-route to Poonch was vitally necessary. It was the only answer to the enemy's tactics.

The Route is Decided

The decision to establish a land link with Poonch was taken; but there were three alternative routes, from which one had to be selected.

One was from Uri via the Haji Pir Pass. This was the shortest route. It was well fortified by the enemy and there was little room to manoeuvre. If pushed through it would entail supplying Poonch from Jammu via Srinagar and Uri, a distance of some three hundred miles, most of which was mountainous.

The second alternative was to make a supply line from Jhangar via Kotli. It was a possible route but the bulk of the enemy forces were concentrated in these areas and Kotli was one of his strongholds.

The third possibility was to supply Poonch from Rajauri via Bhimbar Gali and Mehndar. But there was no road for the full stretch of sixty miles and the approaches had been made almost impregnable, being honeycombed with foxholes and bunkers, evil looking machine-gun nests, booby traps and mines. Indeed Bhimbar Gali had been turned into a veritable fortress.

This last route was the most difficult to establish but would naturally be considered by the enemy as the least likely to be chosen, especially as there was hardly even a track. Because of the many difficulties, it was likely that the enemy would be taken very much by surprise if we chose it. But unlike the first link-up in which our forces had to avoid contact as far as possible and get through as quickly as they could, the new operation would entail heavy fighting; for the enemy had to be thoroughly weakened and cleared from his fighting positions. The rest would depend on the vision, skill, judgment and endurance of the officers and men who were chosen for the task.

Three Knock-out Blows

Before undertaking the link-up operations, we had to deliver three preliminary punches. In this there had to be no sparring or faltering; there could be no halfway measures. Each blow to be given to the enemy had to be a complete knock-out. He had to be thrown completely out of the ring and pushed from the sector he was occupying; otherwise he would later interfere with the column, thereby increasing the hazards already present.

The supply line behind us from Jammu to Rajauri via Naushera and also onwards, as we advanced, had to be made secure (Sketch No. 1).

Firstly, the line from Rajauri northwards to Thana Mandi was feebly held. It had to be strengthened.

Secondly, there was a possibility of a build-up by the enemy in the area around Jhangar which formed a base for enemy pockets, on some of the heights dominating the route from Naushera to Rajauri and which might then interfere with this part of our supply line. This threat had to be neutralised.

Thirdly, the reputedly impregnable Ramgarh fort which had the enemy flag flying over it was at the very gateway to the start of our operations. A little more than four miles north-west of Rajauri, it provided a permanent threat to any land link made from there to Poonch. It would have to be dealt with.

KAILASH VIJAY

As I have mentioned above we were not holding the line between Rajauri and Thana Mandi very strongly. It was known that a regular supply of arms and ammunition was going from Mehndar, cutting eastwards through this line to the enemy at Budil. There, a number of enemy battalions were being formed and trained and raids on our outposts from Budil were also increasing.

In order to deny all possible east and west routes which the enemy could use to maintain and reinforce his stronghold in the Budil area, it was decided to capture Kailash, Point 7710—a height which dominated the whole area overlooking Darhal—and Thana Mandi. By thus severing all possible links between the enemy on the west and his eastern strongholds, we would prevent his forces in Budil from interfering with any column leaving for Poonch. But first we had to by-pass a small enemy stronghold on a hill feature—Point 5570—and to capture high features around it, so isolating it from the rest.

Success depended to a great extent on our carrying out accurate preliminary reconnaissance of the whole sector and the pin-pointing of the position for the final assault. Our seasoned men therefore carried out several patrols deep into the enemy lines and made careful observations. They were to be amply rewarded for the risks taken.

As I have explained, in order to close our proposed barrier against all enemy penetration three features had to be captured *en route* before taking the main objective, Kailash. The Rajputana Rifles and the Kumaon Rifles got down to this task with spirit and enthusiasm.

Setting out at night with Lieutenant General Srinagesh himself keeping in touch with the operation from Rajauri we by-passed the first dominating feature, Point 5570, as planned. For a short distance we had an armoured column of tanks in action, but they could only go a few miles for lack of a road and field guns could not be taken forward for the same reason. Moving swiftly and silently round Point 5570 we went on and captured two hills—Points 5603 and 6454—in spite of sweeping machine-gun and mortar fire. We had now arrived directly opposite our main objective, Kailash, height 7710 ft.

On 22 September the enemy felt the full impact of a frontal assault by the Kumaonis in broad daylight. The battalions were supported by the guns of 7 Mountain Battery, whose Officer Commanding was Capt. Jawala Singh, a lofty, god-fearing man, whose name had become synonymous with guns and noise in our Brigade. Actually his voice was as soft and tremulous, though cheerful, as his guns were loud and accurate. Often I have seen him pat the muzzle of one of his guns as though speaking to it fondly, giving it a *shabash* for the good work it had just done and urging it to keep it up! If William Tell could put an arrow through an apple on his son's head at twenty feet, it is certain that old Jawala could knock one's hat off at two thousand feet with one of his pet artillery-pieces—that is, if he were allowed to try! Of course I am not suggesting that anyone would have been willing to take a chance!

Jawala gave the agile Kumaonis a creeping barrage keeping an accurate hundred yards ahead of them, until they reached a steep incline, when he switched his fire to the crest itself. From our own positions we could clearly see the tiny figures of the Kumaonis, clad in olive green, clawing their way up the steep slopes in full daylight whilst some supporting planes added to the gun barrage with rockets on the summit. Major Chand, the Kumaonis' Officiating Commanding Officer was on the right with his own Company and Captain Kapur on the left with another. There was a hail of machine-gun fire showering on them from above, but the little figures were now halfway up and moving on steadily.

Suddenly the hostiles showed themselves on the crest against the sky, and a shower of hand-grenades came down the slope among the attackers and began to burst in flames and smoke everywhere one looked.

The whole area was still alive with the tat-tat-tat of heavy machine-gun fire. Somehow on the reverse side of the hill many hostiles had avoided the air-strike and our artillery shelling. Fire was coming at our *jawans* from the crests and from the spurs alongside.

The hill was now too steep for artillery to be safely used to shell the positions in front of the men. But they clung to the slopes, ducking as the grenades came down, then lunging onwards again, undaunted by the enemy holocaust.

At this point a cloud obscured the view of the hill but not long after we heard victorious cries of "Kalika Mai ki Jai" as the Kumaonis put in their bayonet charge. Kalika is the goddess of blood and battle against evil. It was the finale. We had begun the battle at midday; we finished it just over three hours later at 3.15. Kailash was in our hands.

Point 5570 which we had previously left untouched was also now taken without much opposition.

Civilians Return

At the completion of the operation the headmen of the local Muslim population, which had abandoned villages in the face of our attack, fleeing to the jungles or on the hills beyond Kailash, returned and contacted Brig. Yadunath Singh with a view to bringing back the people, who had run away, provided they were given every facility to resettle as citizens of the State. This intention of some 25,000 Muslims to return home gave an indication that they had begun to realise the falsehood of enemy propaganda, especially that against the Army, in which they were now eager to place their fate for protection. Lieutenant General Srinagesh, who was present throughout the Kailash operation, left the area with a feeling of considerable satisfaction.

After a conference held with the Brigade Commander, it was decided to build a motorable road through the valley as far as Durhal to maintain the troops in the area, and the Kumaon Rifles, under the command of Major Chand, were put in charge of the entire Durhal and Thana Mandi sectors. It did not take long for Major Chand to win the confidence of the local population by giving them all possible assistance. Eighteen months later when the battalion was to leave this area for good, they received the most touching and spontaneous send-off from the inhabitants.

Having suffered a nasty defeat to the north of Rajauri, the enemy began to reinforce his troops in the areas west and north-west of Chingas—in fact he was trying to cut our supply line in the rear between Naushera and Rajauri. Along this whole thirty-mile stretch, we had only one battalion midway at Chingas. Opposite the line the enemy dominated a number of heights from which he kept sniping and mortaring our troops. Apart from the actual effects of this and the delay it caused in the flow of supplies, it was extremely annoying to our signalmen, for our thirty-mile cable line was repeatedly cut, compelling the lads to examine and repair it time and again while sniping continued—though that was another matter. While such work is normally a routine job it was most harassing, for the men had more than enough to do without having to cope with this disrupting additional work. So when it was subsequently decided that an operation would be undertaken to clear the enemy completely out of the area by capturing Pir Badesar and Bagla, we, of the Signals, were more than pleased.

The Dussehra festival fell on 12 October. The only way our troops could celebrate it was by an exchange of good wishes among themselves and in a few places—a very few—by a *bara khana*. Indeed the festival passed with an increase in vigilance and alertness on the part of the forward picquets; it just came and it went quietly. Only I was more fortunate than most of the troops for, by chance, I got an opportunity to fly to Bombay for my Jewish New Year's Day. I returned well rested and fortified with New Year resolutions: Blood and Thunder!

PIR BADESAR AND BAGLA

Brig. Harbhajan Singh, Commander of 268 Brigade at Jhangar was given the opportunity of carrying out this new offensive, which he launched on 13 October. He set out with a Gurkha battalion through mountainous and trackless country reaching the village of Giran. He caught the enemy asleep. The snores of the sentinels almost drowned the noise made by the column. They were quiet for they were not expecting us and we took the place almost as quietly.

The Punjabs and the Kumaons left this village swiftly and occupied positions around Paran, facing Pir Badesar, their main objective. A number of small features which were taken by the Punjabs had to be consolidated by them. So it was left to the Parachute Kumaons, the battalion of Poonch fame, to storm Pir Badesar supported by rocket-firing Tempests and a terrific barrage from our field and mountain guns as a softening-up process. The Kumaons first made a series of swift and fierce skirmishes and then launched their attack on the feature. Indifferent to the grenades and machine guns, they stormed position after position. Unable to withstand so determined an attack the enemy suddenly turned back and left in disorder, leaving the hill to the gallant Kumaons—themselves inhabitants of the same range of mountains which stretch out towards Nepal and beyond. About one hundred and fifty of the enemy were killed, wounded or taken prisoners in this engagement. Our own casualties were negligible.

After the fall of Pir Badesar the Jats who were at Chingas were ordered to move forward and capture Bagla. Since they had taken Chingas some months earlier, they had been harassed by constant enemy fire. This was the moment for which they had been waiting and they were in no mood to brook any delay. Going headlong into action, they swept aside anything that stood in their way and completed their task within two and a half hours.

The second punch was thus a coordinated double blow. A left hook towards Pir Badesar and a short straight jab into the enemy's middle at Bagla, knocking him headlong from the sector and compelling him to leave our supply route to Rajauri alone and immune from attack. A new cable line was then laid from Naushera to Rajauri and it remained intact without any further interference.

The Situation Eased

By the capture of Pir Badesar the danger to Jhangar was considerably reduced, as the enemy could not concentrate in force without being observed. It also lessened the pressure on our troops in the Naushera sector around the Seri Valley, as Pir Badesar was a height dominating Seri and giving a view even of the Jhelum Bridge and the train movements over it, far away in Pakistan.

The Pir Badesar operation deceived the enemy as well. From the very start this move put him on the wrong scent, giving him the impression that we were heading for Kotli instead of for Poonch. This helped to take the strain off our great Mahratta fighters on sentinel duty on many of the outposts facing the enemy—the same Mahrattas who had played a great part in the famous battle of Naushera in April under the late gallant Brigadier Usman, when over two thousand of the enemy were killed. It also helped to reduce the pressure against the gallant Dogras who had firmly held the positions they captured earlier, keeping day and night vigil under point-blank range of enemy guns, giving as well as taking, until the sledge-hammer blows—Kailash, Pir Badesar and Bagla had been delivered. The fiery Sikhs and Rajputs, some of whom were in this sector too, obtained some respite and were later able to move forward to more advanced positions. And above all, with the success of these preliminaries, the iron jaw of our forces around Jhangar, Naushera, Chingas and Rajauri was slowly but surely closing in a vice-like grip on the enemy.

In the meantime 5 Brigade had come into this sector and taken Pir Kalewa, seven miles north of Rajauri towards Thana Mandi on 28 October. A short, swift but gallant action by the Madras Regiment threw the enemy off this cone-shaped peak.

A Wounded Soldier

I met one of the wounded *jawans* coming out from Pir Kalewa on a stretcher. He belonged to the Madras Regiment and if I remember right, his name was Krishnan Pillai. He had been shot through the shoulder and had a nasty gash there which had been given a first-aid dressing.

I said to him: "How are you, son?"

"Oh, I am all right, sir," he replied with a smile, at which I gave him a nod and looked at him more closely. "Yes, sir," he continued cheerfully as though trying to reassure and remove any suspicion I may have felt, "there is no need to worry; I am quite all right for the bullet went right through and came out at the back. It is nothing, just one of those things which has to occur in battle."

With a lump in my throat and a gentle pressure of his hand I turned away and left him. In my heart I remembered with great satisfaction that this man was not one alone, for such men are found all over the country—they are legion.

The "Impregnable" Ramgarh Fort

The lines of communications having been protected in the rear from Sunderbani to Rajauri, they could have been declared secure enough to start the operations. But a question still remained: would it be of any use starting off on the link-up, for the purpose of establishing a road from Rajauri to Mehndar when at its very gate stood one of its most impregnable positions, a dominating enemy fortress. From this area the enemy would still menace the valley for it was only about four miles directly west of Rajauri.

Plans were therefore set in motion for the formation of our own fortified gate to the land link, by the capture of the fort and the heights around. It was decided to use guile and surprise rather than a frontal attack, by closing a tight ring round the fortress with an unexpected move, thus severing the enemy's supply line (See Sketch No. 2).

The success achieved at Pir Badesar drew a large proportion of the hostiles towards Kotli, which they presumed would be our next objective. The general result was that in strengthening his positions where we appeared to be showing an increase in activity, he weakened his strength in the features around Ramgarh fort. Since our activity had also been spreading along a wide area, he had to stretch his forces and thin out his general line of defence. For though he knew we were going to strike hard, it was impossible for him to defend every hill in the whole area in strength; neither had he the slightest idea where we were going to attack and where he should accordingly concentrate his efforts.

A second temporary (*ad hoc*) Brigade was formed from two units under 19 Infantry Brigade, for, according to the agreement with the UNO, no further expansion in Jammu and Kashmir was allowed. This temporary Brigade was provided with a skeletal staff and with two battalions only—one of the Gurkhas and the other of the Punjab Regiment, also containing a field battery and artillery. This force was called the Rajauri Brigade and was under the Officiating Command of Lt. Col. A. S. Sodhi.

Our operation was planned to be carried out in three phases. First the Gurkha Rifles were to capture three hill features including Naghun, situated about eight miles south to the fort and a similar distance south-west of Rajauri.

In the second phase the same Gurkhas were to move on northwards capturing Point 4956, about two miles south-east of the fort, and Lambi Ridge, a similar distance to the south-west. At the same time the Punjabs were to move up in the centre and attack the fort.

In the third phase the Gurkha Rifles were to push on north of the fort to capture Point 6480, which was the summit of the Neakka forest ridge. This hill commanded miles of country to its west.

On 4 November at dusk, the Gurkhas moved out unobserved from the area south-east of Rajauri covering a distance of about nine miles across hilly country. They arrived at Bathuni forest at about 2.30 a.m. and after taking a breather for an hour, they regrouped themselves one company creeping silently over the thickly wooded hill to Point 4642 which it was able to occupy without opposition.

The second company passed through the first, surprising the enemy who only realised its presence when it was only about thirty yards away. For a short while the enemy put up a stout resistance during which there was much indiscriminate firing and hasty throwing of grenades. But by 9 in the morning it was all over with Naghun in our hands. The enemy had retreated to the third height, Point 4700, from where he continued to snipe and mortar our newly gained positions.

With the enemy rather shaken, the other two companies of the Gurkha Rifles immediately exploited the successes so far achieved. Though under heavy fire from Punjab Gali, Kariyan and Miari forest and from a number of other hills in the Naghun forest, the companies pushed forward swiftly, strongly supported by a heavy barrage from our artillery which soon silenced enemy mortars. Our third objective of the first phase, Point 4770, soon fell into the hands of the Gurkhas, who moved still further towards Punjab Gali capturing everything in their way. Seeing our troops coming through the Naghun sector in what appeared to be considerable strength, the enemy veered his forces round bringing about a brigade to face our battalion and drawing some of his men from the fort for this purpose. So far everything seemed to be going according to plan, for already we had captured our objectives and the enemy was depleting his strength in the immediate vicinity of the fort. But in spite of this early thinning of his forces there, we thought it best to avoid any frontal assault on the fort itself until we had put the second phase of our plan fully into effect.

We intercepted a wireless message from the hostiles in Ramgarh fort which read: "We shall fight to the last man and to the last drop of blood; an oath has been taken by all to this effect on the Koran. Ramgarh fort is impregnable. It shall never fall."

Geographically the fort certainly appeared impregnable. There was a steep incline leading to it, which would be quite unscalable if defended with heavy fire and the enemy in the fort must have been amply stocked with ammunition for a long defence. The only road from the fort led westwards through Lambi forest and he used it to receive his supplies and reinforcements. It was presumably well covered by fire and the fort was certainly in an enviable position where determined defenders could make a long stand.

On 7 November the Punjab Regiment left Rajauri with their forward company heading for Makot Tekri. Two other companies were held up for a while near Niganar, but a swift flanking movement by the fourth company backed by our artillery fire made it possible for them to resume their advance and take possession of the Niganar hill feature, a few miles south-east of Ramgarh fort.

In the afternoon the Gurkha Rifles moved towards a feature south of the fort threatening to cut the enemy's supply route alongside the Lambi Bari Ridge, which was also straffed by Air Force planes and pounded by the artillery. This move which threatened to cut the enemy's only possible route of withdrawal undoubtedly shook his morale.

At this stage the Punjabs swung into action again. They captured Harjilali at dawn next morning and attacked the western end of Lambi Ridge close to the fort. The enemy now became extremely nervous and far more conscious of the danger of his line of communication being cut off completely than of his oath to fight to the last man and to the last drop of blood.

Next the two companies of the sturdy little Gurkhas, that had done so well in the Naghun forest, by-passed the fortress on its east side heading for Point 6480, a dominant feature in the Neakka forest range, north of the fort.

Presuming now that he was surrounded on the south, east and north with our troops well established and still on the move the enemy grew panicky. His one escape route was still open but he knew it would very soon be severed and that if he wished to make use of it he would have to move fast. But though he had not made up his mind to quit when our final assault commenced, the situation certainly had a powerful adverse effect on him.

Soon after dawn on the morning of 8 November, the enemy's discomfiture was increased by our Air Force which began to straff him with rockets, the Tempests swooping like hawks across the half-mile-long fortified ridge, blasting it not only with rockets but with bombs and bullets as well, until thick grey smoke lay across it like a cloud. When they left for their base, the Artillery took over, adding to the smoke and changing the hue of the cloud from its earlier grey to a mixture of burnt-red and black. That short and sharp barrage must have tasted like hell to the hostiles, for it softened them up completely. When the Punjabs made their final onslaught up the hillside at 11.20 they went over the top with wild victorious war cries and captured it without the slightest hesitation.

What a host of fine fighting men there was to choose from in the rank and file of 19 Infantry Brigade. Though the men in each regiment had their own particular characteristics, yet each one seemed to be a bloodier fighter than the other in his eagerness to uphold the honour of his Motherland, and it is not possible to make legitimate comparisons. With us were Gurkhas, Kumaonis, Garhwals and Assamese (Nagas)—all different and yet all related by virtue of the fact that they lived in the same lofty Himalayan range which stretches across the entire northern frontier of India. And like the hillmen there were the tough, sturdy, brave Mahrattas from the Deccan Plateau and those plainsmen too—the Punjabs, Sikhs, Rajputs and Dogras who had for centuries battled against the invaders from the north-west, and are the successors of Porus, Hari Singh Nalwer and Prithvi Raj Chauhan. All were used to the rigours of the climate and fought their battles with the same confidence and in their stride. The people of India can confidently put their faith in these men and others akin to them to protect their Motherland and their flag wherever it flies. Ramgarh fell to our troops at 11.27 a.m. on 9 November. A few days later at a simple ceremony behind its walls the Indian flag was raised to signify our domination throughout the area.

With Ramgarh fort in our hands our strengthened line formed a bulge from Jhangar to Pir Badesar, covering Chingas and Rajauri and passing through Naghun forest onwards to Ramgarh fort and Point 6480 to its north-west. By the establishment of this line, over seven hundred square miles of country had been liberated. The preliminaries to the link-up with Poonch had been completed according to our plan.* We had fulfilled all our expectations to the letter.

On the way to Thana Mandi. Armour goes into action

The author outside a signal office bunker

Artillery training

G.O.C.-in-C. General Srinagesh inspecting an armoured column

A respite

Maj. Gen. Atma Singh, Brigadier (the late Major General) Khanolkar, Major Lee (U.N.O.) and Major Lamba

The Yuvaraj (behind his Yuvarani) with Sheikh Abdullah. Whither destiny!

Gen. Atma Singh and Brig. (now General, grey hair) Yadunath Singh finalising plans at a conference

9

19 Brigade Moves Out

IN the meantime 26 Division moved to Naushera from Jammu and took over all our commitments. 19 Infantry Brigade moved forward to Rajauri and made this place its Base Headquarters. Communications were again reorganised by means of another of the *ad hoc* arrangements we were getting used to. This meant our falling back on the already stretched resources of both the Divisional Signal Regiment and the Brigade Signal Company, Signallers' equipment was included in the term "War Material", which the UNO would not allow into Kashmir except as replacements.

The three Brigades (19, 5 and *Ad Hoc* Rajauri) as well as the Poonch Brigade were all on the same wireless link for both R.T. (Radio Telephony) and C.W. (Continuous Wave—for Morse messages). So each brigade was in direct touch with the other three and with Headquarters, irrespective of its activities or the positions taken up. Poonch was also in direct contact with Rear Headquarters (Durga Force) so that all necessary information regarding operations in their side was obtained first-hand.

Lieutenant Colonel Sen, Commanding Officer, Divisional Signal Regiment, remained at Rajauri doing yeoman service looking after the entire communication network. This officer was mentioned in the despatches—but had I served above him instead of with him, I would have ensured that his boundless energy and devotion to duty was more fittingly acknowledged. Maj. 'Andy' Mehra, who assisted him received the same award.

Lieutenant Colonel Sen was relieved later by Lt. Col. H. K. Bhagwat who carried on the same responsibilities in a quiet and unruffled manner.

A Parting Present

One week before our offensive the enemy could not avoid throwing a parting shot as though he wished to give an indication of events to come. At dusk one day he managed to sneak within range of our Headquarters with his 4.2 inch mortars and gave all he had; shelling non-stop for an hour. Whether it was by design or coincidence, is not known, but all his shells dropped into the Signals Camp area. Seeing us dodge and keep our heads down caused much amusement among the rest of the Brigade personnel, who were watching from a safe distance. Fortunately there were no casualties and, on account of this, we thought it quite polite of him to have thought of us before departing for good. Of course we made the most of this incident by telling the others that the enemy fully realised the value of Signals and was trying to wipe us out in order to disorganise the force.

D-Day Approaches

The 8th of November, the day Ramgarh fort fell to the Punjab Regiment, had been fixed as D-Day for the start of the operations for 19 Infantry Brigade. This was to be known as "Ops Easy". Because of the difficulties expected, it was given a name which our Commanders hoped would have the opposite psychological effect. H-Hour for the attack was dawn. In order to get into position the Brigade had to move out of its camp under the towering pinnacle of Pir Kalewa, two days before, at nightfall on 6 November. The assembly area was in the valley of the Kain

Basān, nine miles west of Rajauri. We had to reach it unobserved by the enemy. From there the first attack would entail another march on the very next night of 7 November, for it had to be completed as a swift surprise move.

On the left flank was the temporarily formed Rajauri Brigade under Lieutenant Colonel Sodhi, Officiating Brigade Commander. On the right flank was 5 Brigade securely entrenched in the Pir Kalewa sector under Brig. Omrao Singh, who had injured his knee in a previous battle and, though limping, was determined to take part in the operation. Though this courageous officer was so reluctant to go back to hospital, he was later compelled to hand over his command as his wound grew steadily worse; and there is no doubt that when he did give up fighting his heart was hurt far more than his wounded knee.

The attacking force was, as we have seen, composed of two normal brigades and one *ad hoc* brigade with a skeletal staff and two battalions. The force's full strength was thus almost that of a division though without many reserves. Reserves could not be made available as due to the UNO restrictions only troops available in the area could go into battle. The combined force was placed under the command of Brig. Yadunath Singh and the formation was temporarily called Durga Force, with its headquarters at the rear. At a conference held by him, the plan was confirmed and the Commander's decision was that 19 Brigade would have to take the brunt of our attack.

The strength of the enemy was known to be at least two divisions and established as they were in defence on almost impregnable heights littered with pill-boxes, bunkers, machine-gun nests and mine-fields, and intersected with unscalable precipices and knife- sharp crests, his actual strength was increased tenfold. The mountainous terrain put him in a formidable position, more than adequately protected against attack.

Brig. Yadunath Singh set about organising the attack in close consultation with Gen. Atma Singh and his own staff officers. Some conferences were held in Jammu with the G.O.C.-in-C. Lieutenant General Srinagesh present.

The Brigadier's Injury

The Brigadier had injured his shin-bone about six months before and had an almost permanent limp. The injury had occurred one day when he suddenly found himself face to face with the enemy only thirty yards away. He had with him his Acting Staff Captain, Bakshi. Using his presence of mind, the Brigadier took off his Gurkha felt hat and shouted to the enemy: "Stop, I am a friend of yours." In the momentary pause of uncertainty and hesitation that followed, he and the Captain were able to jump down an incline and run for their lives under cover of thick forest. He saved himself, but in the process he cut his shin severely.

But in spite of this injury, which was worsening, the Brigadier was still able to keep up with his routine of visits, often climbing miles up and down hills to see his men. There was never any question of his leaving us, for he would refuse point-blank to go back conscious only of the task he had in hand. I fancy that his endurance was the result of the tremendous will power he possessed; or it may have been the result of the yoga that he practised. In any case it was true of this man that, in his enthusiasm to achieve his objective on the battlefield, he gambled with death with the same unconcern that he showed in climbing those hills with his injury. It was all part of his intense devotion to duty which was based on deep patriotism with ultimate desire, perhaps, to make the supreme self-sacrifice—an extension of the creed of personal sacrifice which was his daily practice. Both physically and mentally he was favoured by Dame Fortune; but which successful commander is not? His officers and men were fully conscious of his qualities and followed him eagerly wherever he went, some with reverence, others with blind confidence.

After employing several ruses to deceive the enemy about our intentions and the time of our departure—ruses which appeared to have achieved a measure of success—we left Rajauri at 6 p.m. on 6 November, at the very time when preparations for the attack on Ramgarh fort were under way.

From the abuse he broadcast daily it was obvious that the enemy was fully aware that something was impending, though what it actually was and where our forces would strike was still a matter of conjecture, which kept him on tenterhooks.

Both brigades had already encamped on the Thana Mandi Road, six miles from Rajauri and it was this that led the enemy to assume that we intended to advance; but when we actually left the camp, the tents remained pitched and the personnel of Rear Headquarters were ordered to keep all the lights burning and to make as much noise as possible to give the impression that we were still in occupation.

Equipment Weighed

The Brigade Signal Company had about a dozen mules and a similar number of porters. The mules were only able to carry one hundred and eighty pounds apiece so we took care not to overload or give them extra strain, as we were setting out on a formidable and difficult operation and would have to rely to a great extent on our pack transport throughout. Our signal equipment consisted of wireless sets, batteries, charging engines, telephones and exchange and assault cables, all of which were carefully weighed to the last inch of wire.

Of course all our equipment had to be similarly weighed and it was then I learnt that an army blanket weighs five pounds and was surprised to realise that I had used thirty pounds as my bedclothes during the previous winter, when the temperature was below zero, and still felt it much too light. On this operation each man was allowed two blankets only, one which he carried with him in his pack, the other being mounted on the mules. The second blanket could only be used when the mules caught us up, for they generally took a different route. The average temperature when we started the operation was only two or there degrees above freezing point and it was getting colder daily; also there was generally a stiff, biting wind blowing on the tops of the hills where we always seemed to be. My men, mostly Madrasis, intelligent and quick-witted soldiers who made up most of the technical units in the area, never thought anything of it and took it in their stride—much better than I did. Winter clothing was of course worn all the time, with woollen scarves serving as improvised headgear. Turned inside out and rolled over twice, these made queer-looking Balaclava caps which when pulled over the ears did succeed in producing at least an illusion of warmth.

In Jammu and Kashmir snow generally begins to fall about the beginning of December—sometimes earlier—though on many of the heights in the Himalayan region it snows for eight months in the year; and on features over 23,000 ft. there is usually perpetual snow. Unlike other places in India rain falls heavily in winter in Kashmir and these winter rains added to our discomfiture. Since the "Ops Easy" was scheduled to take twenty-one days, it was a race against time so far as the weather was concerned and the margin was a very narrow one.

Our stores included a quantity of Paludrine. We also took a chemical preparation which was spread on our woollen battle-dress and which minimised the possibility of its tearing if it was not washed within fourteen days. This chemical was also poisonous to ticks which was important since typhus was known to be prevalent in the area.

Respect for Property

Before leaving we were given strict orders, which were made very clear indeed to the troops, that not a single shack or house or anything within was to be touched. There was to be no burning of buildings or property of any description, for every dwelling would be needed for the rehabilitation of over half a million Muslims of the vicinity who, misled by enemy propaganda, had fled across the border unwittingly bringing untold suffering on themselves. So far as we were concerned, all civilians were to be treated courteously and given assistance wherever possible. It was made clear that strict disciplinary action would be taken against anyone contravening these orders. But as it was, our men had no wish or thought of doing anything else and the orders need hardly have been given.

Since Brig. Yadunath Singh was officiating as the overall Commander of Durga Force, Lt. Col. Jagjit Singh was appointed to officiate in his place as 19 Infantry Brigade Commander. After making a detailed appreciation of the situation, the Colonel issued instructions that wireless operators would have to carry their sets in addition to their own weapons and packs, while going forward into battle, since porters were liable to panic under fire. The wireless sets weighed anything from twenty-seven to sixty pounds and the batteries, so essential, weighed up to ninety-seven pounds each. Of course the heavier batteries (175 ampere hour) were required only for the CN 348, a set through which the Air Force could be contacted. But in any case during these operations, men who had to keep going at a fighting pace carried much more weight for a much longer time than had been done on any previous occasion—even in the campaigns during World War II. And this is not forgetting the fact that, after this enormous physical effort of carrying heavy weights, our signallers had to get down to receiving and despatching messages at every halt, which meant no small mental effort and consequently very little effective physical rest. But these men of ours fully realised the need of the moment and invariably got down to their task with eagerness.

Mishaps in the Dark

We reached the assembly area after an all-night march in darkness. It was precipitous country and the mules delayed us; in fact one of the units lost a couple of animals which disappeared into a five hundred-foot deep ravine. Indeed one officer, Major Wright, who was by now well known for his gallantry, also stumbled in the dark and fell eighteen feet injuring his leg badly. He had to go to hospital, but later he literally ran away from it in order to return to his battalion in time for the final battle. This was typical of the morale of all our officers and men.

A conference of all officers commanding units of 19 Infantry

Brigade was held in the assembly area below a knoll, overlooking enemy territory. The plan was re-affirmed.

It was known before setting out that the enemy was in strength in the area east of Rajauri. To make a frontal attack would mean delay and unnecessary waste of life and accordingly, as we have seen in the previous chapter, the newly formed Rajauri Brigade under Lieutenant Colonel Sodhi had begun its own operation two days before D-Day and was to fight its way forward in the Naghun valley towards Ramgarh fort, thus diverting much of the enemy's attention towards this likely objective. With this major diversion going on well to the west, 19 Infantry Brigade was to circumvent Bhimbar Gali sweeping swiftly in an arc to capture the dominating heights along the south-west side of the valley, from where it was to continue towards Poonch.

"B" Echelon

According to the plan, all supplies and ammunition required were to be dropped by air after the first three days, for there was no road. The engineers had a herculean task ahead of them in building one over such mountainous country and no matter how fast they progressed, they would never be able to keep up with the speed of the operations, which were scheduled to last for not more than eighteen days. All the requirements of the Brigade were signalled to the rear by wireless. The dropping of the necessary equipment at the exact place selected and at the right time depended, to no small extent, on the information being sent correctly and in time. As there was many an item of equipment required urgently on the same day as the signal was handed in, the messages had to be passed on swiftly and accurately. Contact would then be made promptly with the Air Force and the material brought by air either from Jammu, Srinagar or Pathankot, as was most convenient.

We were always in radio telephonic communication with the Air Force. There was never once a failure. The airmen played their part magnificently and on no occasion was anything that was required ever delayed. They invariably acted at once. The reply to our messages was always "Roger Roger", or "Wilco", technical terms for "O.K. message understood" and "Will comply". And they did comply. To the lads with the wings and all of their Force we said many a "Thank you", small words but offered as a token of much sincere appreciation and gratitude. If for success, mutual understanding and sympathy are required between an Air Force and an Army, there was no reason for failure from this cause in Jammu and Kashmir.

"B" Echelon consisted of the Brigade's reserve equipment and supplies carried on mules accompanied by only a few men. The party had to take a circuitous route as there was no continuous road or track running in our direction. In fact the going was so difficult, that the party of engineers accompanying them was often required to cut a way across rocky outcrops and other difficult places for this column. The task of Major Gill, who was in charge of these mules and men, was undeniably tedious and since we did not expect to see him for stretches of 48 hours at a time, we always took with us three days' rations—one day's cooked; one day's uncooked and *shakarpara* biscuits for the third day. Also with "B" Echelon went our J.C.O., Jemadar Nair, in charge of the Signal Group.

Though we had marched all through the night of 6 November, we spent most of the day at work in reorganising. We had laid a cable up to the assembly area and were thus in telephonic communication with Rajauri Headquarters. Our intention was to continue laying the line with the forward battalion and to await developments. It was thin assault-cable and there was a loss of more than three decibels per mile, which meant in theory that the voice would not be audible over a distance greater than ten miles. However, we thought the result would be worth the effort, which was all the more since the line had to be laid away from the route or track taken by the column, to avoid the possibility of its being snapped by the troops or broken later by the mules. It proved more than worth the trouble and this line served another useful purpose in marking a track for those who got lost or diverted from their way, for it gave an indication of the route the Headquarters had taken.

10

Into the Fray

AT dusk on 7 November we set out from the assembly area going over the lower hump of a saddle on to the Hyatpura range with the Kumaons, under Lt. Col. Dharam Singh, in the lead. It was a long thinly spaced line, shadowy and ghost-like, silently shuffling its way forward through obstructing shrubs and thickets and winding its way in and out, in a snake-like column. We were now in enemy controlled territory. Soon after dusk it became pitch dark for even the starlight was obscured by a mantle of clouds. It was difficult to see an individual more than a yard or two ahead yet, to know if he was there, one had only to stretch out a hand.

There was no smoking and no talking—not even whispering; for we knew that in the stillness of the night and in the clean, clear mountain air the slightest untoward sound could reach the enemy. We were right in their midst, and here and there hardly three or four furlongs away, we would pass enemy shacks with lights burning in them. Often the silence of the night would be broken by the barking of a dog or the call of a jackal, which would be taken up in a howling chorus by its mates, reaching a crescendo before suddenly fading into the distance, with the night again settling down in sinister silence. We would pause apprehensively, but the lights in these shacks would continue to burn, showing us that all was well and that no suspicion had been aroused. The only audible sound remaining would be the sighing of the pine trees swaying to and fro. And we would continue in our snake-like formation right under the muzzles of the enemy guns and mortars, keen, eager, excited, concerned only in pushing on to our objective. What the near future held for each one of us, no one could guess. No one could tell what even the next hour had in store, for many miles still lay between us and our objective.

A Message in the Night

And as we kept approaching nearer and nearer to battle, we could hear the distant melancholy strains of the *veena* twanging musically over the mountain tops. Mingling tunefully with the rustle of the pine leaves and the sound of the rippling river from far below it would reach us ever so softly, singing in time with the pounding rhythm of the *tabla* thumping across from the same direction, far away. It was refreshing. Was it coming from the camp? Was it a message that we were in the thoughts of those left behind, urging us to keep going?

It was easy to lose one's way. Our men, saddled with wireless sets had to slow their pace when going down an incline, losing valuable seconds which meant being separated twenty or thirty yards from the men in front. A *jawan* taking a wireless set had to be twice as careful as one carrying a light machine gun or rifle for, owing to the frail internal structure of the set, it might easily stop functioning if he happened to trip over. With a control set to the forward battalions out of commission or with any other link broken, there would be a partial breakdown of communications which might result in much confusion, putting many lives in jeopardy. We could take only one reserve set with Main Headquarters the other being mounted on the mules with "B" Echelon, which at times was not likely to reach us for at least three days, because of the roundabout route it had to take. Thus each operator was compelled to tread more cautiously than any other man, particularly in the dark. On him and his actions depended so many others.

The river was crossed at Dheri Dhera and the column moved forward towards Bhimbar Gali. Being right down in the *nullah* with hills around, all the wireless sets of the artillery, engineers and signals experienced "dead screening" at times, the wireless signals being unable to get through because of the steepness of the hills around, which had a gradient of one in four.

Forward of Dheri Dhera the battle began.

The first task was the capture of a height—Point 6307—to neutralise Bhimbar Gali, which was a virtual fortress. The enemy had prepared strong pill-boxes covering all the approaches along the spur to the summit. The Kumaons went into the attack against the continuous crump crump of mortar and automatic fire yet, nothing daunted, they swept along in two-up formation until compelled to scale, in single file, a track which overlooked a direct two hundred-foot drop into the swiftly raging torrent of the river flowing below. When a grenade burst among them, one or two were seen to fall and roll down into the torrent, for no wounded man could cling to such a steep slope. It was tragic. But it was only a small part of Life's panorama on the battlefield.

Notwithstanding the secure position of the enemy, Lt. Col. Dharam Singh and his little men forced home the attack; five times they were held, and five times they charged with bayonets fixed, eventually dislodging the enemy from their fox-holes and throwing them over the reverse side of the slope. As the light of morning began to dawn on 8 November the first feature had fallen to us. The action had been fought by the regiment single-handed, without artillery support; it was an achievement of great courage and determination.

Two other features were taken by the Rajputana Rifles—Points 6207 and 6274, which not only covered the left flank but gave us a clear view of the Thurti valley, six miles south of Mehndar. A gathering of about a thousand hostiles presented an ideal target for our guns. After the first few shots the enemy fled in disorder, leaving about sixty killed.

The First Phase Concluded

To bring the first phase to a successful conclusion, the main feature we had still to capture was Point 6944, three miles south of Bhimbar Gali. It was first hoped that the engineers might be able to push through a rough road fast enough for field guns to be brought into action here; but owing to the rocky and mountainous terrain, it proved a tremendous task and they could not keep pace with the infantry. Neither was there a "mule-able" track anywhere on these unfrequented Himalayan heights. There were some paths shown on the age-old maps, but often enough these had long ago been encroached on by undergrowth and trees through which a new track had to be hewed. This kept the engineers busy, hacking, smashing and blasting until a usable mule track was completed through this virgin Himalayan region, to enable a battery of mountain guns, and 25 pounders under Maj. K. M. Chinappa, to be brought up in time.

Our Headquarters was mortared from Point 6944 which the enemy held in strength, and we suffered slight casualties. But what we felt most was the loss of a few porters who deserted. Their behaviour was understandable since they were never trained to stand up to fire; besides for them there was the thought that only twenty miles in the rear were their wives and families who must have been waiting and anxiously wondering what was happening, for they were still well within the sound of the guns. To these simple porters life had all its value in just living as a part of the family. But for us their desertion meant more strain on the already over-stretched resources of our men.

Lt. Col. Jagjit Singh made a reconnaissance towards Point 6944 with Captain Gear, the Intelligence Officer, and his Brigade Major. The attack was going to be no picnic, for it was to be made in daylight, and the enemy were prepared and waiting for it. They must have felt that it was about time they held our advance somewhere, and it was on this feature they decided to do so.

But our friend Chinappa, backed by the Air Force and the ground troops, the Punjabs, had other ideas. Under his direction and observation, disconcerting balls of fire were poured accurately on to the height while the Air Force rocketed the hill. Then, at half-past five, the Punjabs, who had slowly crept up into position, charged with their bayonets glittering in the late afternoon sun. The enemy, after stubbornly trying to hold on, cracked up at the sight of cold steel and fled in terror. The victory sign, a blue Verey light, was fired within one hour of the start of the attack.

The First Chance to Rest

19 Infantry Brigade had now marched about twenty miles within the last few hours, up and downhill over crests and precipices, fighting most of the way. At three in the early hours of the 9th morning, our men got their first opportunity to lie down after 65 hours' activity. Most of us lay down to rest where we were on the rocky ground in our battle-dress of course—all except those who kept guard and were on duty on the wireless sets. These were relieved after two-hour shifts.

The whole of the Main Headquarters Signals had now become a part of Tactical Headquarters which moved forward at the speed of the fighting with all its equipment and batteries. Batteries weighing seventy-seven and ninety-seven pounds, which could not be entrusted to the care of the porters now for fear that they might fall out on the way for a rest, had to be shouldered uphill most of the time by our operators, the remainder of the signalmen carrying loads not much less. And even after such exhaustive marches, during which the men's endurance was fully tried out, the signalmen knew no respite when a halt was called, for as usual they had to busy themselves immediately with the reception and transmission of messages.

These alternative periods of physical and mental exertion continued throughout the twenty-one days of the operation. It was a contingency that had never been witnessed before, either in the Burma Campaign, in Frontier warfare, or even in the earlier days of the Jammu and Kashmir operations. No operators had been called upon to undergo such continued strain for so long a period as twenty-one days. Yet it was done eagerly and successfully.

The Battery Problem

In operations as mobile as these were, without vehicle transport, battery-charging facilities were negligible. The use of the batteries had therefore to be carefully restricted, because a group of two batteries (which are required for one of these army sets) lasts about three hours and only one pair could be taken in reserve. Unless a definite time limit is given for an operation, which is not always feasible, the signal officer may have to insist that his sets be switched off for certain periods, depending on the urgency of the situation. But though this would only be resorted to in an emergency, it might well be the lesser of two evils. But at the same time it is very necessary to keep the staff fully informed regarding any such decision.

Instead of the sets being kept switched on continuously with the battery power being steadily used up, possibly without many messages being passed, a scheduled working-time of fifteen minutes every hour can be an alternative. Certainly no commander, under the stress of battle, could tolerate or could be made to understand a cessation of wireless communication due to lack of battery power.

The lines we laid were constantly cut by enemy artillery fire and sometimes by our own animal pack transport. On occasions it was difficult to avoid laying lines across or along tracks and thus having them cut unintentionally or tripped over by troops. Often, however, there was no track when the line was laid originally, but since carrying or stretcher-parties going up and down later were inclined to follow the cable, they often made tracks along the cable route.

All these difficulties demanded continuous long hours on the part of operators and linemen who, in addition, had frequently to face heavy fire while laying and repairing lines. And on top of all this there were no reinforcements to replace casualties, as in every section all Divisional or Brigade personnel were fully occupied.

On the 9th morning the Signals were required to accompany Brigade Headquarters and one battalion on a small operation to assist Rajauri Brigade about six miles away on the left flank and, after connecting up with them, to take Point 6360. With the Parachute Kumaons under Lt.Col. Dharam Singh, the job was completed in double-quick time. We then returned.

It was after seventy hours on the go, near Point 6944, that we dropped down two hundred feet to a small blue stream, clear and cold, flowing between rocky banks. Here we bathed and rested for a while on the shore where pines whispered in the wind. Beneath the trees the earth was cool and clean and from all around came the fresh fragrance of pine leaves and the green grass that grew in abundance about us. Soon we were at work again cleaning and maintaining our weapons and equipment.

Activity Increases

All units carried out intense patrolling from here. Small disorganised parties of the enemy were met and dealt with and the day brought in a good haul of prisoners, arms and ammunition. Activity was on the increase in all sectors. Units from Thana Mandi pushed forward slightly while Rajauri Brigade, which had taken Ramgarh fort and 268 Brigade from Pir Badesar, made simultaneous thrusts towards Kotli intensifying their patrolling towards this city.

19 Brigade's move in taking Point 6944 still gave no indication of our intention of swerving towards Poonch and the enemy line was being further and further stretched and thinned out, since they were expecting us to strike towards Kotli in a concentrated attack. Every deceptive move made so far had achieved its purpose by putting the enemy off and keeping him guessing.

19 Brigade was formed up ready for the next hop. Gen. Atma Singh paid us a visit and congratulated all concerned on the work already done. He expressed pleasure at the manner in which operations had been conducted so far and commented on the excellence of the all-round signal communications, which had enabled him to contact whomsoever he wanted without delay. Even the atmospherics had behaved themselves!

While with us the General was presented a captured rifle by

some officers as a memento. Before starting back to Rajauri with his staff officer, Lt. W. Carvalho, he handed over the rifle to a prisoner, Ghulam Mohammad, with whom he had a long and friendly chat. This was typical of this campaign throughout which there was not the slightest ill-feeling nor hostility shown towards any of the prisoners. They were treated all the time almost as though they were our own men and their presence was taken most naturally and unconcernedly by all our troops. The prisoner who was handed the rifle could easily have made use of it as a club, if not as a gun, for the General was unarmed. But by putting his trust in the prisoner, he made it clear that it was not blood that we were out for but only the attainment of our ideals and, in this particular case, the achievement of an object—to form a land link with the garrison and population of Poonch.

By now, with all the rough going, we were beginning to feel ravenously hungry but around us there was nothing but deserted houses, fields of chillies and a number of stray sheep that were grazing close at hand. Of course we had our dry rations to eat, *shakarpara* biscuits and so on, but no one could deny that there could be nothing better than a good hot meal. We had no condiments with us and had lost our salt, as the sack had been split open by a splinter from a mortar shell and our reserves were with "B" Echelon which had not yet caught up. We therefore took our meal "off the land"! Without much compunction we got hold of one of those wild woolly sheep and soon had him boiling merrily with some chillies for seasoning! We were so hungry that we really enjoyed it—salt or no salt. It was good, it put new life into us, and I personally felt like letting go a real good Tarzan yell; but this might have given the hostiles a warning of our whereabouts, so on second thoughts I kept quiet—silence was the better part of valour.

Our next meal was the same. But already the palatability of boiled meat, saltless and with no curry-powder, was definitely decreasing, so we sent an S.O.S. to the Air Force, who were hovering over us, for some condiments. That very day they dropped some real hot *masala* brought specially for us. In fact it was so hot it kept us running for a week! But that did not matter for it was still very welcome. Again our thanks went out to the Air Force.

Enemy Cooperation

Major Gill, the Quartermaster with "B" Echelon, now joined us and the enemy seemed to take a particular delight in causing interference whenever he had to speak on the wireless set. For about two days they would keep coming up on our wavelengths jamming our link to the Division. Sometimes they would release a flow of abuse either at Major Gill or the Indian leaders and their families. Gill would then turn to me, the Signal Officer, for assistance in getting the message through. What I tried was to call the enemy station in the following manner:

"Hullo Operator *Dushman* (enemy), Pronto speaking." (Pronto was a code term for the Signal Officer which was known to both sides, as it was in use under the British before Partition). "Pronto speaking. I have a message to pass. Will you please stop interference. Over."

My idea worked. The enemy came back on the air: "Hullo Pronto, Hullo Pronto, this is not your *dushman*, but your friend. Wilco, Wilco. Pass the Message, but do so yourself. Over."

Being a "Q" message, it sometimes took more than twenty minutes to put over on radio telephony, but it had to go. Whether these operators knew me before Partition, or because the word *dushman* had the exact opposite psychological reaction, or whether they liked the tone of my voice, I cannot say, but they carried out my instructions on several occasions as though we were both on the same side. And at times, if I was too busy to pass a message myself, I would tell them so, to which they would reply: "Roger, Roger (understood) OK." It was certainly good of them. Eventually, by various means, we eluded this enemy station, or rather avoided interference.

The Trustworthy Prisoner

There were a number of prisoners at Headquarters and I was surprised to see the amount of kindness being shown to them. I have related the story of Gen. Atma Singh and the rifle. Well, these prisoners often gave assistance with the equipment, and those of our officers who were responsible for their security seemed to be more concerned about their welfare than that of our own men. On one occasion one of the prisoners actually had the audacity to ask for four days' leave in order to bring his family back to the area! I expected him to get a refusal but to my astonishment he was given permission. The prisoner kept his word, though he took six days to find our Headquarters which was by then in a different place.

5 Brigade had captured their objectives, Point 5073 and a small hillock north-west of Mehndar, according to schedule and without much opposition. During the night of 10–11 November, one column moved out against Height 5732 at 2.00 a.m. The Punjabs put in an attack but the enemy was well entrenched and held out. Making a reconnaissance we found that to attack Point 5732 from the east would entail a long detour, while the approach from the north-west was so narrow that it would allow little or no room for manoeuvre. The only alternative in the circumstances was a frontal attack which would entail a series of point-to-point actions in a bid to come up close to the enemy before finally storming his positions. The only objection which weighed heavily against this plan was the unacceptable delay involved, since speed was the essence of the whole operation.

At midnight on 13 November, while we were lying in the open, the enemy suddenly opened up with his guns apparently without first registering our positions, for his fire was inaccurate and concentrated well behind us. We could hear the shells whistling as they hurtled past and exploded harmlessly in the valley a short distance off. A few stray shells which landed amidst us burst ineffectively without causing damage—as though the hand of Providence guided those shells to preserve all from harm.

Lt. Col. Jagjit Singh then made a split-second decision. He decided to hold on to his former positions on Point 6944. After consulting the Force Commander and Gen. Atma Singh, he gave orders to manoeuvre around to the right flank on to Hill 5073 in order to reinforce 5 Brigade's success.

Had we attacked 5732 and captured it, we would have then come up against further enemy positions on excellent defensive terrain at Jhika Gali, Gold and other features. These were strongly held in a convex arc-shaped line stretching from the south-west to the north-east of Mehndar and would have resulted in numerous sharp engagements and delay. Indeed we intercepted an enemy message reading: "Gold feature will be defended at all cost. Stop. Otherwise political repercussions expected." Though whether they were able to carry out this order was soon to be realised.

Eventually by making a swift sweeping movement in a fierce left-hook drive, almost encircling the enemy rather than giving short and direct punches, we secured handsome dividends. Though life was not to be thrown away heedlessly it was not of paramount importance in this engagement. The task to be achieved was that formulated by the country. It was her plan, her very own: "The Poonch Garrison will be relieved." That was all, but to us it was sufficient. The greatest factor to be considered was time. In less than a fortnight these very hills, on which we were situated, would be covered by over ten feet of snow accompanied by the blizzards and rains characteristic of the Himalayan region. Thus there was a possibility, nay a certainty, that the operations would be bogged down, or develop into a terrible winter campaign, if we were delayed.

The swift diversion of our forces also brought the morale of the enemy to a new low ebb; for he was already badly shaken due to our successes in other parts of the area. That he was becoming confused and worried there was every indication. On the night of 14 November we were facing him on the south-west of Mehndar and on the very next day the whole force, less one battalion, was nowhere in the vicinity. If by chance he had any idea of our new position, he would have found that from the south-west of Mehndar we had turned up on his north-east. Whether he was informed or not we were unable to say. But by his firing or trigger-finger nervousness throughout the night on an imaginary foe and unprotected posts—as seen by his lighted tracer bullets—we knew definitely that we had him worried.

Therefore the decision to reinforce 5 Brigade's success, made by Lt. Col. Jagjit Singh backed up by Brig. Yadunath Singh,

A welcome invasion! Reinforcements!

A moment of cheer in Kashmir. A day at the races with the ladies

Congratulations from Gen. Atma Singh to Brig. Yadunath Singh — signifying the link-up

showed sound reasoning under the circumstances. It was a demonstration of flexibility in battle and confidence in our ability to shift without the assistance of mechanised transport, almost as swiftly and as silently as though manoeuvring on a chess board. That the men and officers would live up to that expectation there was never the slightest doubt. Lt. Col. Jagjit Singh himself had given not only a display of good judgment but of confidence in his men's ability to carry out his orders. His handling of the operation together with that of his Brigade Major, Gurdas Singh, was extremely sound.

It was at this juncture that Col. Kuldip Singh (now Brigadier) joined the Brigade, remaining for the rest of the operations.

A Disappointed Battalion

The battalion that was left behind opposite Point 5732 was to demonstrate towards the enemy, probe his defences and generally keep him on edge. The regiment chosen was the Rajputana Rifles. Seldom have I seen men look so hurt and dejected as the officers and men of this battalion. They seemed completely taken aback for they were being left out of the operation. There were even some tears. And if ever a man can be justified and excused for a display of the weaker side of his nature in a show of tears, it is then and then only, when he considers that he is being done out of a battle for his country.

In such fine fettle were these lads, so tense, so eager to spring forward, that had they been given the word to advance there and then, even without support, nothing could have stopped them—neither hell fire nor high water. But the time was not yet ripe. When, later, the word to attack was flashed the reaction was electrical. Fixing their bayonets, shouting their war cries, and scrambling almost in a frenzy, yet in orderly fashion, over hill and dale, they took one feature after another overstepping their real objective, advancing too far and too fast! But this is a later story.

Years ago, as a youngster, I remember seeing a bull terrier straining at the leash in an effort to break loose. When we left the

Rajputana Rifles at Point 5732 my thoughts flew back to that moment. There was little difference, except that these men were held back by what we knew as "orders"! Such is discipline that it neither showeth nor alloweth a display of personal feelings. How those men felt and how much it hurt them they alone knew. But I could understand, for I was their Signal Officer, in close touch with all.

We left Point 6944 in the same winding formation. We stalked through Bhimbar Gali and over the hump after dusk, appearing phantom-like in the dim luminosity of the rising crescent moon. With this light the figures and the ground were visible for over fifteen yards, enabling us to distinguish the type of ground we were scrambling over; we avoided tripping and rolling over as had happened on so many occasions before. But we maintained the same strict discipline, with no smoking and no bantering, for we could now hear the continuous rattle of machine guns and the barking of mortars went on throughout the night as the enemy kept vainly searching with desultory fire trying to discover our position. "B" Echelon with the mule column was now following immediately in our rear.

By our brilliant and rapid movement we succeeded in outflanking the enemy and driving him precipitately north-west. The face of the whole operation had therefore shifted completely from one side of Mehndar to the other.

On Point 5073, with 5 Brigade, we organised punches for the final push. Here we were visited by a number of VIPs and Commanding Officers, all eager to see the latest for themselves, and to give and exchange views; officers from the Medical, Ordnance, Supply, Engineer, Animal Transport and other Infantry units, all came.

Gen. Atma Singh, as usual, made the most of the opportunity to visit his men. It was his regular habit and often he would appear at almost every picquet. The higher a hill or the steeper a feature, the more pleasure he seemed to find in climbing it, if his men were at the top.

General Srinagesh, with one or two of his staff officers, was there sitting on a rock, pondering over the latest plans. He was an officer who quickly won the hearts of his men for his quiet and unassuming manner; yet one who got things done in a determined and forceful way with an eye for detailed planning and organisation. No more need be said but that it was instinctively felt that one day he would be of the greatest service to the nation—even after his military career. However, that is left to the future to prove.

Signals at Work

In the meantime we got a few "drops" of signal cable from the air. On our way over Bhimbar Gali we met some of our own men from Rajauri who had been instructed to come up with a couple of wireless sets which we changed. We also received a high-powered telephone, and made arrangements to pick up the mail—to everyone's pleasure. A regular schedule was fixed for the letters to be brought daily to the front lines on mules.

The RT (Radio Telephony) net to the Poonch and Rajauri Brigades was manned by a hard-working youngster, Lance Naik Velu Nair (now a Naik, the equivalent of a Corporal), who was reluctant to receive any assistance, and stayed with his wireless set all the time. Rod aerial was used and reception was exceedingly clear.

Then there was Naik Mohammed who controlled the vital forward links to the battalions, also seldom allowing himself any relaxation.

In mountainous areas the range of sets is reduced and particular attention has to be paid to their sitting, which is an important factor. This he did most intelligently, always advising his operators with the forward battalions to advantage.

On every occasion radio-telephonic contact was established between fighter and bomber aircraft and our Army wireless set on the ground, with useful results. To make a success of this type of contact, wireless sets must be accurately tuned to the given frequency and both pilots and the Army ground stations should have their hearts in the job. Lance Naik Santa Nand, who was responsible for the Army set, CN 348, with its two heavy batteries weighing over ninety pounds each, did a very fine job supervising and man-packing the equipment up and down the rugged, hilly terrain without the slightest damage. His cheerful voice made him many friends among the pilots.

Then there was Lance Naik Mohammed Ishak who, manning the exchange, appeared happy only when his trunk-lines were through. These were sometimes damaged by shelling and if the General happened to ask for a call when the line was out of order, he would ring him up as soon as it was through and say something like this: "Sir, the line damaged by shelling has been repaired for your call within forty-five minutes. Your call is now through, sir." And the General would carry on, with a smile.

I must also mention Havildar Thayain who maintained the wireless sets from the battalions, repairing them almost as fast as they came in. And Havildar Abraham, who had joined the Brigade Section seven years earlier, was always ready with a cheery word of encouragement—he was the N.C.O. in charge.

The cipher operators, like the others, had to get down in the dark during the halts to work throughout the night enciphering and deciphering with the light of a dim torch behind some cover or in a trench. There were only two of them with us; one was Havildar Ranbir Singh who had contracted fever practically from the start but who would not return until his relief came. When he did go back, he left mounted on a mule for he was too ill to walk. He weighed a good 180 lbs. He was quite a veteran and rather dejected about having to leave us.

Well nigh five thousand groups (words) were passed daily on wireless and twelve hundred of them on cipher, in spite of the fact that half the time was spent in marching and battling. Many groups were done in semi-dim light, the operators encoding or decoding stretched out on their stomachs. Each man knew his task and carried it out to the best of his ability, each conscious of his responsibility and reluctant to share it with any other. They were a fine set of *jawans*, all Madrasis, intelligent, quick to grasp things, and hard-working, who had gone through much battle experience in various spheres of the world—the Middle East,

Sicily and Italy in World War II—and were now doing their bit in operations for their own country.

But one factor that assisted us a great deal was the way the staff officers passed information and instructions to each other, forward and to the rear, by radio telephone during battle. This cut down our signal messages by at least two thousand groups a day. Strict station discipline, security and carefully worded instructions were noteworthy features in these conversations, which gave nothing away to the enemy. Lapses in wireless procedure and bad wireless discipline are a source of very valuable information to an enemy wireless intelligence service. It was fortunate that our staff was well versed and experienced in radio-telephony procedure, maintaining a standard which could only be achieved by constant practice and training.

11

The Road Goes Through

HOUR for the final onslaught was dawn on 21 November, 1948. Intensive patrolling was carried out to probe the enemy's defences. The tempo of operations was accelerated and a few short, successful attacks were carried out to improve our positions.

The two Infantry Brigades, 19 and 5, advancing from the south were now poised, grim and tense, for the last attacks. There were two features to capture on our side: Topa Ridge (Point 5055) and Point 5982 (see Sketch No. 4).

Poonch Brigade under Brig. Pritam Singh, marching from the north towards us, were prepared and lined up. Utilising whatever forces they could muster they had captured one hill after another until only the last and strongest enemy foothold was left to conquer, Marghot Ghazi, 6876 ft. high.

Orders of the Government of India

Every one of the commanding officers in the two brigades was summoned to a conference, to receive the last and final briefing. Brig. Yadunath Singh, standing with his feet astride facing north, pointed towards Topa Ridge, the last enemy stronghold still in our way. Raising his voice and speaking more vehemently than he had ever been known to do before, he said:

"Gentlemen, you see those two features in front of you; they must be captured at any cost and it will be done, even if all of us have to give our lives to do so. These are not my orders, and neither are they those of the General Officer Commanding-in-Chief, nor of the Commander-in-Chief himself." "No," he said, pausing to emphasise his point, "they are the orders of our Government, the Government of India—of our own country. The land link with Poonch will be pushed through. The population will be relieved. That is all."

There was little need to say more, for he knew his men—no commander could wish for any better. The plan had been given out earlier. 19 Brigade was to capture Topa Ridge, and 5 Brigade was to cover the right flank and take Point 5982. Poonch Brigade was to begin operations simultaneously and take 6876.

Urgent and emergency top-secret signal messages were flashed back and forth between Poonch Brigade, ourselves and Durga Force Headquarters at Rajauri; they were checked and rechecked and sometimes sent to Jammu and Delhi—high-level Headquarters. Nothing was left to chance. It was a co-ordinated attack to go in on schedule, timed with precision. It had to be successful.

I called up my men and put them completely in the picture, repeating the words of the Commander. All of them were in fine trim. Communications were perfect, and everything was well set. The whole of Brigade Headquarters was on its toes, eager for the word "Go".

The Final Onslaught

Dead on time and in pitch darkness the force slipped out, silently and unobserved from its position, in separate waves and in the directions decided on. The task had been begun. The Punjab Battalion from our Brigade started off almost at the double. Uphill and downhill they moved according to plan. First four thousand feet up; then down to two thousand feet once, twice;

then up again to six thousand feet; then at last they swept forward with bayonets pointing at the enemy. Yelling hoarse war cries, with the "do or die" tone clearly distinguishable and reverberating round the rugged hills in a rising crescendo, they charged and stormed one crest after another, smashing through everything in front of them. They reached the final spur with their victorious war cries resounding again and again. "What could stay that tide of frenzy? No, not human flesh."

The enemy broke and fled in panic in all directions, screaming, leaving behind much booty, mortars, mortar bombs, shells, rifles, ammunition, blankets and even their mules in their hurry to get out of the way of this mad onrush.

5 Brigade had also achieved its objective while Poonch Brigade had forced the issue with four bayonet charges.

This last battle for Poonch was fought on 21 November. Exactly one year earlier in 1947, the Indian Army had entered Poonch with one battalion. Now on the same date, 21 November, 1948, the Army had linked up with Poonch—fighting a gallant action. Yes, 21 November was certainly Poonch Day in every respect.

Brig. Yadunath Singh, in the lead, did not wait very long but carried on alone in the darkness of the night, after 5 Brigade had taken its objective. He nearly paid with his life for his over-enthusiasm, for no message had gone out that he had left to meet the Poonch Brigade Commander personally. He was going under the guns of our own troops who had not been informed about his intentions. After one or two warning shots from his own men, he fortunately realised that it was safer to remain still than to move about, and so huddled down in a hole at the bottom of a hill he shivered in the cold, biting wind of the oncoming winter. The men above him, suspecting that there was something suspicious lurking about below remained, quiet but alert, waiting for the light of dawn to find out what it was.

But when the Brigadier's absence was later noticed, a signal was radioed telling everyone of his excursion into the night. A detachment was sent out from the Poonch side to look for him and it did not take long to recognise his characteristic pose, waving out to them in his Gurkha felt hat.

Following closely on the heels of the investigating section was Brig. Pritam Singh. At once the two Commanders, light of step and glad of heart, approached one another and met in a firm clasp of hands signifying at long last that a land link had been established from Poonch to Rajauri–Naushera–Jammu and to India! Many a man from amongst us was soon to go through marching in victoriously to be reunited with his wife, family and loved ones left behind, as it seemed, so long ago.

But the full task was not completed yet. The lines of communications behind our present positions had to be entirely cleared of the enemy, since they were still on one or two hills overlooking Mehndar from the east near Jhika Gali and the Gold feature. Some mopping-up remained to be done.

RAJPUT FURY UNLEASHED

It will be remembered that the Rajputana Rifles had been left behind and were still opposite Point 5732, glaring hard at the enemy confronting them since it was they who were the cause of the present static rôle of the regiment during these final operations—and the men found it hard to forget this. The battalion had been ordered to stay there to keep the enemy jittery, and the *jawans* were now themselves getting restless, for much time had elapsed and they were eager to get on and do some fighting before the operation was completely over.

19 Brigade was now on Topa Ridge—exactly north of Point 5732, Jhika Gali and the Gold feature—while the Rajputana Rifles were south of them. All that was left was for the pincer to close.

Contacting the Rajputana Rifles on wireless the exact time was set for the commencement of the final move. Their objective was Point 5732 along with other hills in the vicinity. We were to advance towards them from the opposite side, taking the heights on their north and mopping-up all enemy-pockets of resistance.

When the word "Go" was flashed to them—there was little need to give it twice—they moved so fast that in almost the same stride they took Point 5732, Jhika Gali and the Gold feature, and the impetus of their onrush carried them beyond their objectives.

The Commanding Officer who had just taken over the battalion was Lt. Col. Irwin Singh Kuller, now a Brigadier. He was a brilliant officer who had adopted the name "Irwin" in memory of a great friend of his, a British officer, Captain Irwin, who was killed in Burma during World War II, in operations in which both took part.

His men had to be stopped. I spoke to Major Lamba, his second-in-command, personally by radio-telephony, and told him in no polite terms to halt immediately. For in their over-enthusiasm to surge forward those men would soon have been attacking us, as we came in from the opposite direction. The battalion was pulled up with a jerk. There were no more heights to capture or clear. The task had been completed.

But if those men had almost run into their friends, the spirit that drove them can be understood. For the first time in over a hundred years our *jawans* were in the battle not as mercenaries, but as free soldiers, fighting for their own kith and kin; and what is finer than fighting for one's Motherland? So who can blame them for their eagerness? Their morale was great. They were determined, as their action showed, not to be left out at any post.

The morale of the enemy was shattered. He left much booty behind and made little effort to stop our onslaught, fleeing in complete panic and disorder all around. Kotli, formerly one of the strongest enemy bases in Kashmir, was now absolutely empty and the enemy were still running. It was ours for the asking—and behind it even up to the border. We had only to walk in to take it. The matter was mentioned in conversation amongst ourselves. Many a thought flashed through our minds about carrying on until orders came to halt. But the country had to abide by its word to UNO. Only the relief land link to Poonch was contemplated and no more. We halted . . .

During the year of fighting from November 1947 to November 1948, that gallant Poonch garrison, enclosed and overcrowded in a tiny area of ten square miles, threw back and broke up more than two hundred assaults, killing and wounding over six thousand of the raiders. And they were always encouraged and inspired by the grim determination of the men, women and children of the city whose sheer will to exist, to live and to attain freedom in their own homes and from the very hearths of those homes, could achieve naught else but survival through victory.

Poonch! Its history had become an immortal saga of courage, endurance and tenacity of purpose, inspired by the Army and written in the blood of those people of Kashmir. Today it is an epic that will never fade from memory.

We Mortals Humbled

The rains came seven days later. They fell in torrents, accompanied intermittently by heavy snow, without a pause for fifteen whole days; blizzards and bitterly cold winds lashed against us in all their might, piercing the body like the sharp edge of a blade, as though the gods of the elements, having held back for so long to allow mankind to complete its whim, felt now that it was well-nigh time to vent their wrath upon the living. They did so with characteristic Himalayan fury—incessantly and ruthlessly. Nature feels not, nor cares for the pangs and discomfiture undergone by humanity on whom it wreaks its frenzy whensoever it wishes. And the biting driving rain continued unabated, challenging as though fully aware that there was no power amongst us weather-beaten mortals to stay its hand. We, those mortals, remained subdued and humbled; humbled until the frenzy of Nature had spent itself in its own fury.

But though we had completed our task before these rains, the weather had been up against us all at times and our men were hardened to it as this strange story shows.

On one occasion a Company came from a high feature which was covered with ten feet of snow and where the temperature was twenty degrees below zero, in order to establish its headquarters in a more favourable position. It happened, however, that the Company had completely forgotten to bring down one of its outposts consisting of a havildar and three men. The havildar, who had not received orders to leave, forged around and found some rum. This kept the detachment happy for a few days without rations which had been consumed much earlier. It was not till the rum had been finished that the N.C.O. began to get worried, though not about the rations yet. So, calling one of his men he said: "Go down to Headquarters and find out what has happened to the Company Quartermaster Havildar; just tell him to send up more rum."

Needless to say the Officer Commanding the Company woke up with a start to learn about the forgotten section, ordered the men to come down and allowed a generous issue of rum on their return.

Then there was the occasion, a little earlier, before the closure of the operation, when we had received a message giving the information that a frozen-crested peak, 17,400 ft. high and not far from us, had been climbed and captured by troops under General Thimayya's Command in a blinding snow-storm, where men halting for ten minutes could get frozen.

General Thimayya's men had also hurled out the enemy, taking much booty, in extraordinary places. Indeed, scaling in rarified air where men find difficulty in breathing because of the lack of oxygen and where each step taken requires a double effort, Zojila Pass, on the way to Leh, had been captured. In fact the feats accomplished in the capture of Zojila Pass have provided an astonishing new chapter in the story of Kashmir, which, if and when written, will surely be acclaimed as one more great epic of the colourful achievements of the country—a fascinating story I may tell one day.

The Brigadier Departs

Immediately on the completion of this particular operation, Brig. Yadunath Singh was given firm orders by the General and the doctors to leave the area on account of the injury to his leg. He did so, handing over to his successor, Brig. V. R. Khanolkar. He remained in the military hospital at Delhi for three months. One day in Agra, a year and a half later, his car flashed past me while I was on my way to duty. It stopped sharply with a sharp screeching of brakes, for the Brigadier had recognised me. Rushing out of the car, he approached me and put his arms around me in the traditional Rajput manner. Physically he had changed, putting on about twenty pounds in weight, but at heart he was exactly the same, having the same regard for the men and officers who had served with him.

From him I had borrowed a number of books on yoga and philosophy as well as a biography of Swami Vivekananda. I had taken them while in the operational area before he left. I now availed myself of this opportunity to return the books during his stay in the station.

It was left to Brigadier Khanolkar to carry on the good work done and to consolidate the line, reorganising the whole area. He was followed by his staff and men with the same enthusiasm, keenness and discipline as had become characteristic of the Army in Kashmir. The Brigadier himself showed a loyalty not only to his seniors but also to those under him, displaying a quality not found in many.

On 1 January 1949 Gen. Atma Singh went up with a number of us to Kailash for lunch. It was a respite that we were allowing ourselves on New Year's Day.

After lunch, at ten past two, we were sitting down having a quiet conversation, while the General and Lieutenant Colonel Dhillon were playing bridge with two other officers, when a telephone call came through from the GI, Lieutenant Colonel Pande at Naushera. He instructed an officer to tell the General that there would be a cease-fire that night, and that all troops were to observe it and stop fighting or patrolling.

There were about a dozen of us present when this news came over. Though it was a complete surprise there was not a comment made. It was received in absolute silence. The General continued with his bridge. We carried on with our interrupted conversation. Half an hour later, after his game was finished, the General, who was a popular after-dinner speaker, stood up and said only these words, quietly but stirringly:

"Gentlemen—India will be a great country. Be loyal to her."

That was a solemn moment, high up on Kailash, surrounded by the beauty and majesty of the lofty snow-capped mountains which seemed symbolic of our thoughts at the time.

Standing there amidst those white, dignified pinnacles and gazing far across them, each with his own solitary thoughts, we officers raised our glasses, and in one voice replied:

"INDIA".

Index

Abraham (Havildar), 102
2 Airborne Divisional Signal Regiment, 15
8 Animal Transport Regiment, 39
26 (2 Airborne) Divisional Signals Regiment, 28

"B Echelon", 86–7, 89, 95, 96, 100
Bafliaz, 42–3
Bagla, 70, 71–2
Bailey suspension bridge, 56
Bandipur, 27
Banihal Pass, 4, 5, 26
Baramula, 2, 4, 5, 7, 10, 17, 27, 29, 32, 36, 63
Barty, D., 44
Beripattan, 6, 52, 56, 57
Bhag, 65
Bhagat, B. S. (Brigadier), 29, 30
Bhagwat, H. K. (Lieutenant Colonel), 80
Bhimbar/Bhimbar Gali, 6, 49, 50, 66, 86, 90, 91
19 Brigade Signals, 53–5
  equipment, 83
161 Brigade Signals, 26
163 Brigade, 30
  Signal Section, 26, 48
268 Brigade, 94
  Signal Section, 33
  Bren guns, 2
Budil, 67
Burma, 108
  Campaign, 34, 92
Butcher (General), 28

Cariappa, K. M. (Lieutenant General, General), 19, 28, 53, 56, 57, 62
Carvalho, W. (Lieutenant), 95
Chakoti, 63
Chand (Major), 39, 69, 70
Chinappa, K. M. (Major), 91
Chingas, 52, 70, 71, 72
CN 348, 85, 101
C.W., 79

Dakotas, 3–4, 24–5, 31–2, 44
Darhal/Durhal, 67, 70
Dheri Dhera, 90
Dheri-ki-Gali, 42
Dhillon (Lieutenant Colonel), 39, 40, 42, 50, 111
Dogras, 17, 72
Domel-Baramula road, 2
19 Divisional Signal Regiment, 15, 28, 29, 30
Durga Force, 79, 81, 85, 105
Dussehra festival, 70–1

Eisenhower (General), 13
"Errands of Mercy", 61

Ferris, L. E. R. B. (Major), 3

Gear, D. (Captain), 60, 91
Gilgit, 5
Gill (Major), 87, 96
Giran, 71
Gold, 98, 107–8
Gurkha Rifles, 74–5, 76

Haji Pir Pass, 17, 63, 66
Harjilali, 76

Height (Point) 5732, 97, 99, 107–8
Himalayas, 9, 13, 30, 46
  blizzards, 14, 19, 109
  snowfall, 84
  tracks, 91
Hyatpura, 88
Hyderabad, 35, 60

Independence, 1
Indian National Airways, 28
Instrument of Accession, 2
5 Infantry Brigade, 73, 79, 81, 97, 98, 100, 104, 105, 106
19 Infantry Brigade, 28, 39, 49, 61, 85–6, 92, 104, 105, 107
  rank and file, 77–8
19 Infantry Division, 28
19 Infantry Brigade Signal Company, 52
26 Infantry Division, 28
161 Infantry Brigade, 3, 17, 30
Irwin (Captain), 108
Ishak, Mohammed (Lance Naik), 102
Italy, 13, 102

Jammu, 2, 5–7
Jat Regiment, 50, 71
Jhangar, 6, 7, 28, 56, 66, 67, 72, 73, 78
Jhelum, 63
Jhika Gali, 98, 107–8

Kahuta, 17
Kailash, 69, 70, 72, 112
Kain Basān, 80–1
Kalika, 69
Kallar defile, 40
Kaman Gosha Gali, 6
Kapur (Captain), 69
Kariyan, 75
Kashmir
  defence of, 2–5
  in normal times, 10
  Maharaja of, 2
  snowfall, 84
  valley of, 28, 30
  war, 1–14
  war equipment, 30, 54–7, 79
Kashmir State Forces, 2, 6, 16
Katoch (Brigadier), 30
Khanolkar, V. R. (Brigadier), 110
Khargil, 28
Kot, 6
Kotli, 6, 63, 66, 72, 74
Krishnan Pillai, 73
Kuller, Irwin Singh (Lieutenant Colonel), 108
Kumaon Regiment, 17
Kumaon Rifles, 39, 46, 68, 70
Kunial–di-Gali, 50
Kuriyan, P. K. (Major), 17

Ladakh Valley, 30–2
Lamba (Major), 108
Lambi Ridge/Lambi Bari Ridge, 74, 75, 76
Leh, 28, 61, 110
  see also Ladakh Valley

Madras Regiment, 73
Madrasis, 83–4, 102
Maharajpur Ridge, 41
Mahratta fighters, 72, 77
Mahura, 2
Makot Tekri, 76
Marghot Ghazi, 104
Medical Corps, 57
Mehndar, 37, 43, 63, 66, 90
Mehra, Andy' (Major), 80
Miari, 75
Middle East, 102
Miransaheb, 33
Mirpur, 2, 6, 7
Mohammad, Ghulam, 95
Mohammed (Naik), 101
mountain warfare, 11–14
Muree, 63

Muzaffarabad, 6
7 Mountain Battery, 68

Nair (Jemadar), 42, 87
Nair, Velu (Lance Naik), 101
Naghun, 74, 75, 86
Nambardars, 41
Namdev Power (Sapper), 57
Narayan (Havildar), 55
Naushera, 6, 52, 56, 67, 70, 72, 73, 79, 107, 111
Neakka, 75, 76
Nehru, 11, 28
Niganar, 76
North Korea, 13

"Operations Grain", 20–3, 35
"Operation Gulab", 41, 42, 47, 50
"Operation Hail", 50
"Ops Easy", 80, 84

Pakistan, 2, 3, 6, 11, 33–4, 65
  see also Rawalpindi, Jhelum and Murree
Pakistan Signals, 34
Paludrine, 84
Pande (Lieutenant Colonel), 111
Parachute Kumaon Battalion, 35, 39, 43, 46, 49, 71, 88, 90, 94
Paran, 71
Partition, 1, 2, 3
Patel, Sardar Vallabhbhai, 11
Pathankot, 15, 29, 86
Pir Badesar, 70, 71–2, 74, 78, 94
Pir Kalewa, 73, 80, 81
Pir Punjal, 4
Point 4642, 75
Point 4700, 75
Point 4770, 75
Point 4956, 74
Point 5073, 97, 100
Point 5570, 67, 68
Point 5603, 68
Point 5875, 41
Point 5982, 104, 105
Point 6207, 90
Point 6274, 90
Point 6307, 90
Point 6454, 68
Point 6480, 75, 76, 78
Point 6876, 105
Point 6944, 91, 94, 100
Point 7710, 67, 68
Poonch
  city of, 10–25, 63
  final relief of, 61–2
  garrison of, 35, 108
  intrusion of raiders, 2
  land link with, 65–78, 95, 107
  men and women, 9–10, 46
  story of, 7–8
Poonch Brigade, 49, 79, 101, 104, 105, 106
  Communications, 48
Poonch Day, 106
Punjab Battalion, 105
Punjab Gali, 75
Punjab Regiment, 39, 40–1, 46, 50, 74, 76, 80

Radio Telephony, 79, 101
Rajauri, 6, 10, 36, 37, 40
  land routes, 66, 67, 72, 73–4, 107
Rajauri Brigade, 74, 79, 81, 86, 93–4
Rajputana Rifles, 40–1, 50, 68, 90, 99, 107
Ram, Babu (Signalman), 28
Ramgarh fort, 67, 73–8, 80, 82, 86, 94
Randhawa, P. S. (Captain), 26
Rawalpindi, 63
refugees, 1, 3, 11, 18–19, 22, 47
Riasi, 6
Royal Indian Army Supply Corps, 55

Santanand (Lance Naik), 101

Sen, L. P. (Lieutenant Colonel, Brigadier), 17, 30, 79–80
Seri, 52
Seri Valley, 72
shakarpara, 46, 87, 95
Sicily, 13, 102
Singh, Atma (Major General, General), 28, 45, 47, 53, 60, 81, 94, 96, 100, 111
Singh, Bhan (Signalman), 28
Singh, Dharam (Lieutenant Colonel), 88, 90, 94
Singh, Gurdas (Brigade Major), 99
Singh, Gurdev (Second Lieutenant), 26, 48
Singh, Harbaksh (Brigadier), 30
Singh, Harbhajan (Brigadier), 71
Singh, Jagjit (Lieutenant Colonel), 39, 85, 91, 97, 98, 99
Singh, Jawala (Captain), 68
Singh, Kuldip (Colonel), 99
Singh, Kulwant (General), 26, 28
Singh, Mehar (Air Commodore, Group Captain), 20, 24, 31–2
Singh, Omrao (Brigadier), 81
Singh, Pritam (Lieutenant Colonel, Brigadier), 15, 17–18, 19, 21, 23, 35, 43, 45, 104, 107
Singh, Promodh (Lance Naik), 27
Singh, Ram (Lieutenant), 39
Singh, Ranbir (Havildar), 102
Singh, Yadunath (Brigadier), 41, 52–3, 60, 69, 81, 85, 98, 104, 106, 110
Skardu, 29
Sialkot, 33
Siot, 41
Sodhi, A. S. (Lieutenant Colonel), 74, 81, 86
Srinagar, 16, 63, 66
  communications in, 26–7
  defence of, 2–5
  Nehru's visit to, 28
  threatened, 2
Srinagar Divisional Signal Regiment, 15
Srinagesh (Lieutenant General, General), 53, 68, 70, 81, 100
Standstill Agreement, 2
Suchetgarh, 33
Suleman (Major), 15, 19
Suleman, Mohammad (Major), 34
Sunderbani, 52, 73

Tempests, 71, 77
TEWTS, 60
Thana Mandi, 40, 41, 67, 70, 73, 83, 94
Thayain (Havildar), 102
Thimayya (General), 28–9, 30–2, 110
Thopa Ridge, 46
Topa Ridge (Point 5055), 104, 105, 107
Tunisia, 13

UNO, 74, 79, 81, 108
Uri, 5, 7, 17, 26, 27, 28, 29, 30, 66
Usman, Mohammad (Brigadier), 6, 39, 72

World War II, 13, 29, 34, 85, 102, 108
Wright (Major), 85
Wynne, T. (Flight Lieutenant), 15

Zojila Pass, 28, 61, 110

SKETCH No. 1

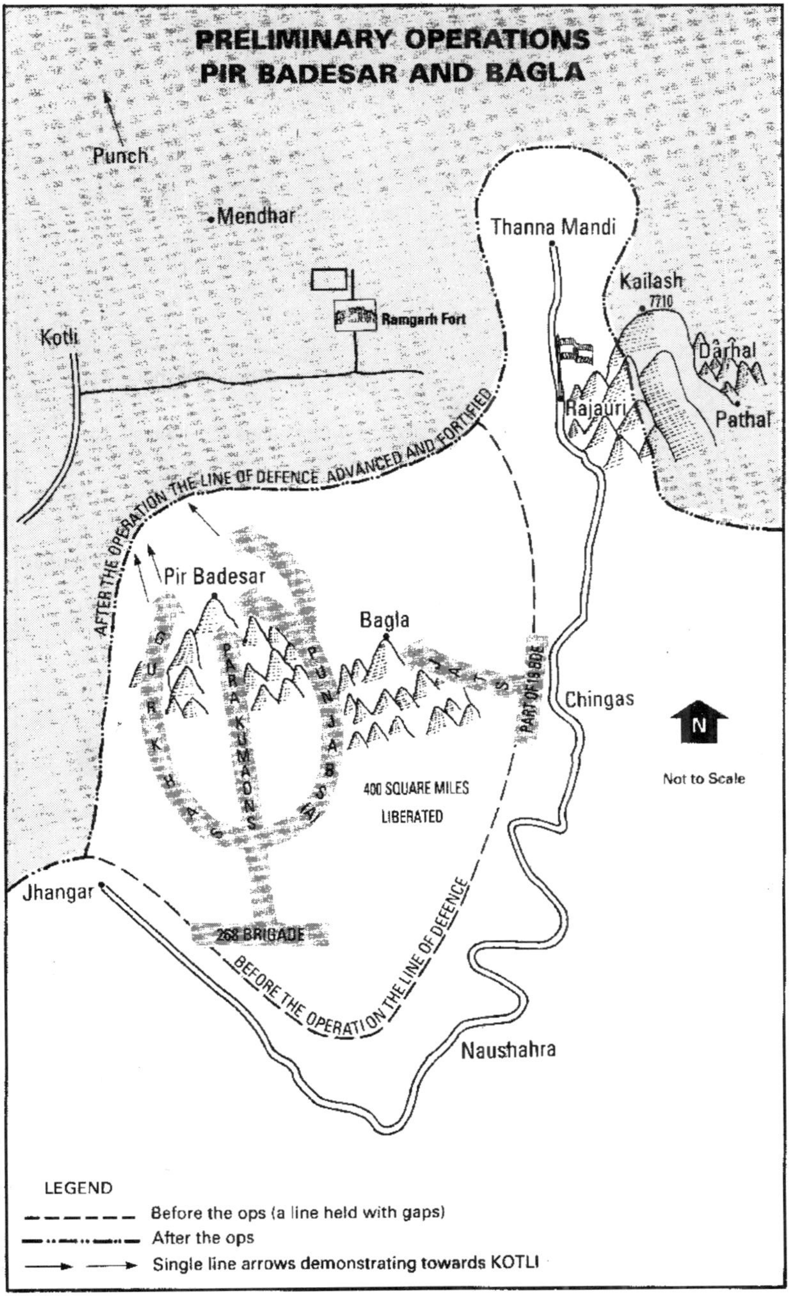
PRELIMINARY OPERATIONS
PIR BADESAR AND BAGLA
Punch
Mendhar
Ramgarh Fort
Kotli
Thanna Mandi
Kailash
7710
Darhal
Rajauri
Pathal
AFTER THE OPERATION THE LINE OF DEFENCE ADVANCED AND FORTIFIED
Pir Badesar
Bagla
GURKHAS
PARA KUMAONS
PUNJABS (A)
JATS
PART OF 19 BDE
Chingas
N
Not to Scale
400 SQUARE MILES
LIBERATED
Jhangar
268 BRIGADE
BEFORE THE OPERATION THE LINE OF DEFENCE
Naushahra
LEGEND
Before the ops (a line held with gaps)
After the ops
Single line arrows demonstrating towards KOTLI

SKETCH No. 2

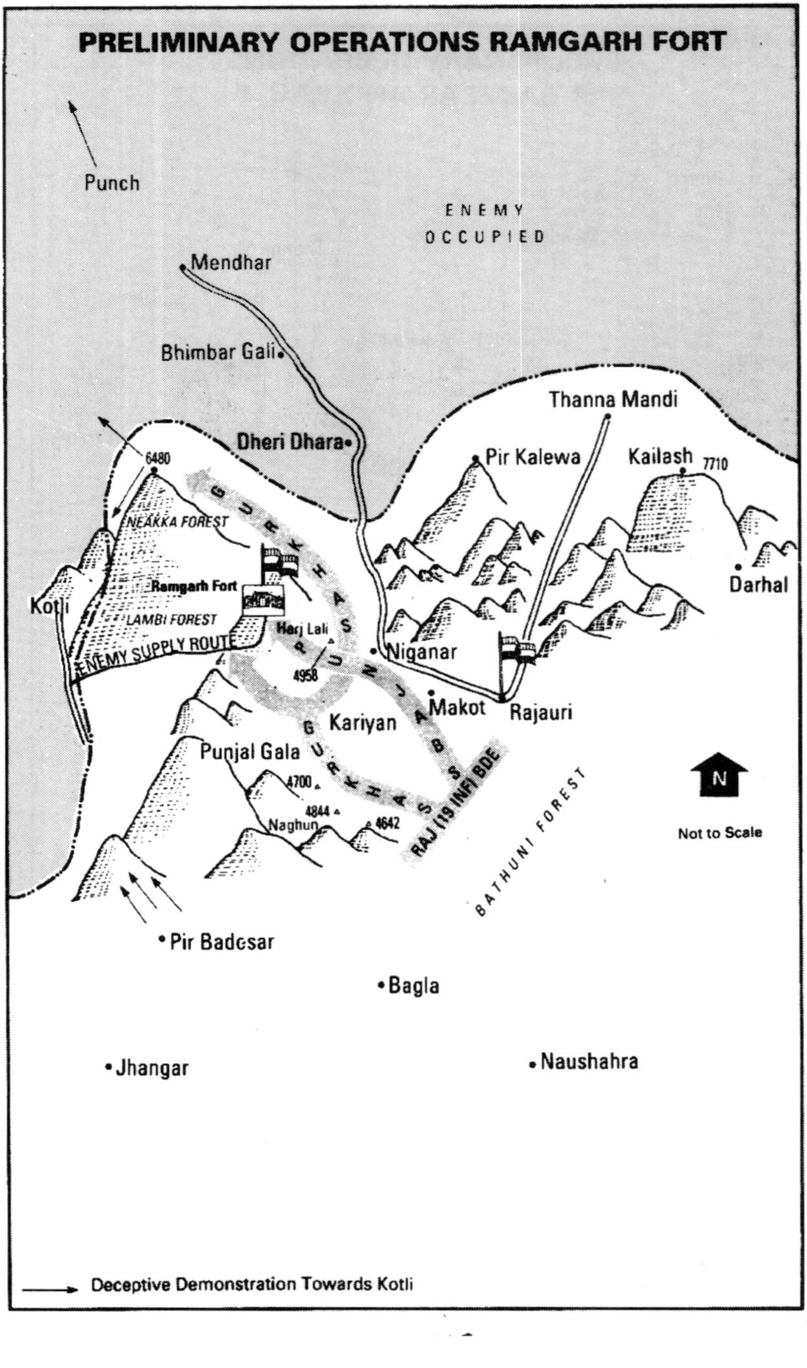
PRELIMINARY OPERATIONS RAMGARH FORT
Punch
ENEMY
OCCUPIED
Mendhar
Bhimbar Gali
Dheri Dhara
Thanna Mandi
Pir Kalewa
Kailash
7710
6480
NEAKKA FOREST
Ramgarh Fort
LAMBI FOREST
Kotli
ENEMY SUPPLY ROUTE
Harj Lali
4958
Niganar
Makot
Rajauri
Darhal
GURKHAS
PUNJAB
Kariyan
Punjal Gala
GURKHAS
4700
4844
Naghun
4642
RAJ (19 INF) BDE
BATHUNI FOREST
N
Not to Scale
Pir Badesar
Bagla
Jhangar
Naushahra
Deceptive Demonstration Towards Kotli

SKETCH No. 3

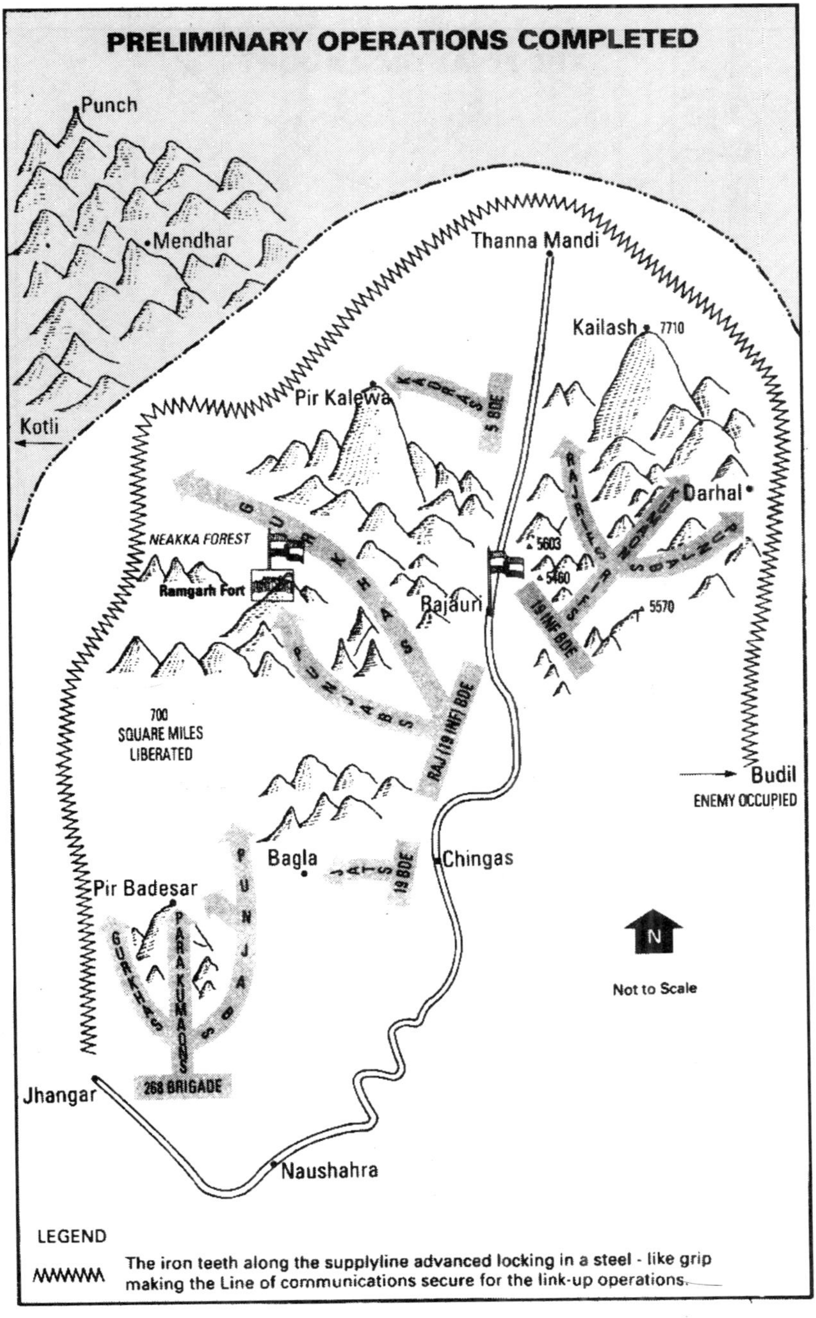
PRELIMINARY OPERATIONS COMPLETED
Punch
Mendhar
Kotli
Thanna Mandi
Kailash 7710
Pir Kalewa
KADRAS
5 BDE
GURKHAS
NEAKKA FOREST
Ramgarh Fort
Bajauri
5603
5460
5570
Darhal
RAJRIFS
19 INF BDE
PUNJABS
RAJ (19 INF) BDE
700
SQUARE MILES
LIBERATED
Budil
ENEMY OCCUPIED
Bagla
JATS
19 BDE
Chingas
Pir Badesar
PUNJABS
GURKHAS
PARA KUMAONS
268 BRIGADE
N
Not to Scale
Jhangar
Naushahra
LEGEND
The iron teeth along the supplyline advanced locking in a steel - like grip
making the Line of communications secure for the link-up operations.

SKETCH No.4

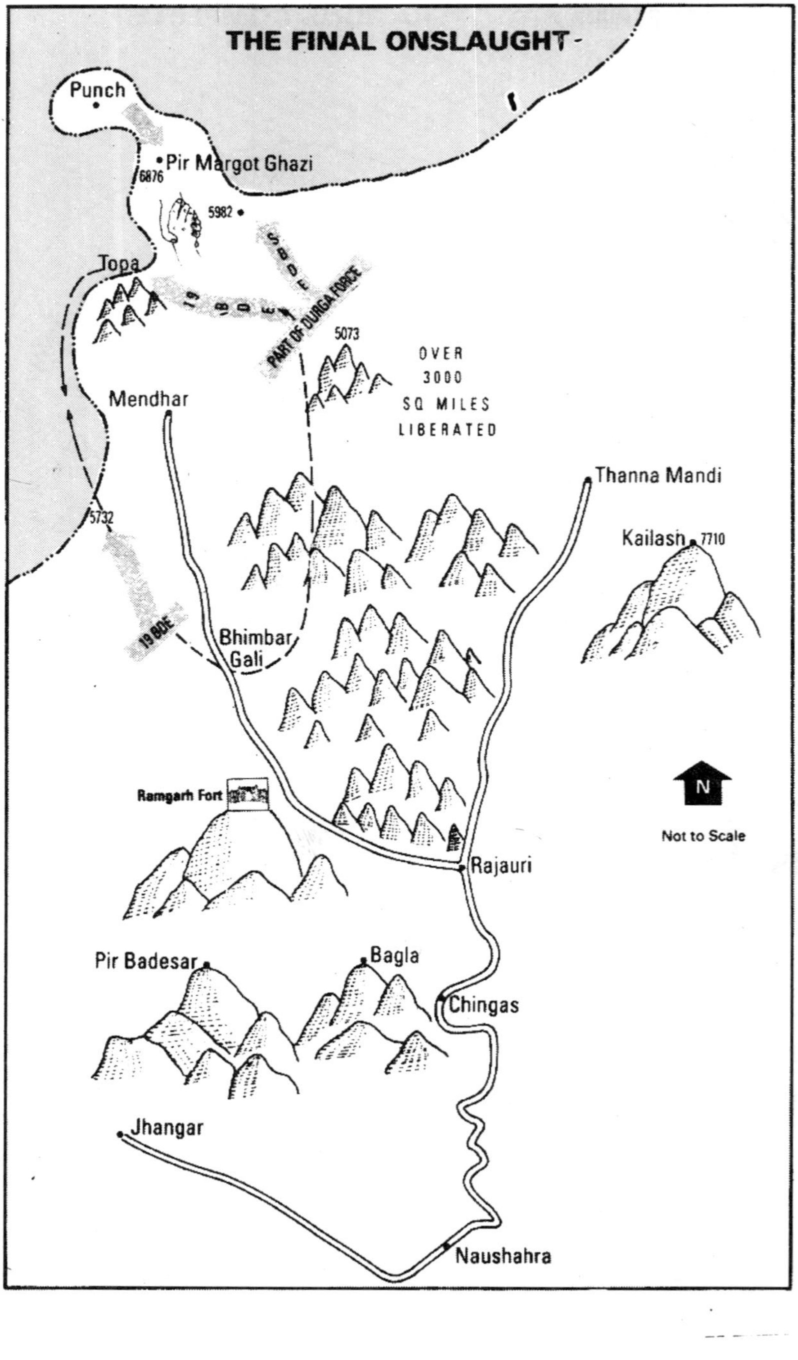
THE FINAL ONSLAUGHT
Punch
Pir Margot Ghazi
6876
5982
5 BDE
PART OF DURGA FORCE
Topa
19 BDE
5073
OVER
3000
SQ MILES
LIBERATED
Mendhar
Thanna Mandi
Kailash 7710
5732
19 BDE
Bhimbar
Gali
N
Ramgarh Fort
Not to Scale
Rajauri
Pir Badesar
Bagla
Chingas
Jhangar
Naushahra